The Miter Fits Just Fine

Carol
Heres something
Written about one
of our favorites —
Enjoy

With all my love,
Pam

COWLEY PUBLICATIONS is a ministry of the brothers of the Society of Saint John the Evangelist, a monastic order in the Episcopal Church. Our mission is to provide books and resources for those seeking spiritual and theological formation. Cowley Publications is committed to developing a new generation of writers and teachers who will encourage people to think and pray in new ways about spirituality, reconciliation, and the future.

The Miter Fits Just Fine

A Story About The Right Reverend
Barbara Clementine Harris, Suffragan Bishop,
Diocese Of Massachusetts

by Mark Francisco Bozzuti-Jones

Published in the United States of America by Cowley Publications, a division of the Society of Saint John the Evangelist. No portion of this book may be reproduced, stored in or introduced into a retrieval system, or transmitted, in any form or by any means—including photocopying— without the prior written permission of Cowley Publications, except in the case of brief quotations embedded in critical articles and reviews.

Library of Congress Cataloging-in-Publication Data:
Bozzuti-Jones, Mark Francisco, 1966-
    The miter fits just fine : a story about the Rt. Rev. Barbara
    Clementine Harris, suffragan bishop, Diocese of Massachusetts /
    Mark Francisco Bozzuti-Jones.
         p. cm.
Summary: Describes the life of Barbara C. Harris, an African American,
and the first woman to be ordained a bishop in the Anglican Communion.
    ISBN 1-56101-220-3 (pbk. : alk. paper)
    1. Harris, Barbara C. (Barbara Clementine)—Juvenile literature.
2. Episcopal Church—Bishops—Biography—Juvenile literature. 3. African
American women clergy—Biography—Juvenile literature. 4. Episcopal
Church. Diocese of Massachusetts—Biography—Juvenile literature.
[1. Harris, Barbara C. (Barbara Clementine) 2. Episcopal Church—Clergy.
3. Bishops. 4. African Americans—Biography. 5. Women—Biography.]
I. Title.
    BX5995.H345B69 2003
    283'.092—dc22

                    2003014118

Scripture quotations are taken from *The New Revised Standard Version of the Bible*, © 1989, by the Division of Christian Education of the National Council of the Churches of Christ in the United States of America. Used by permission.

Cover art: Photograph ©1989 by David Zadig. Barbara C. Harris at her Consecration. Pictured with her mother, Beatrice Harris (now deceased).

Cover design: Jennifer Hopcroft

This book was printed in the United States of America on acid-free paper.

Cowley Publications
907 Massachusetts Ave.
Cambridge, Massachusetts 02139
800-225-1534 • www.cowley.org

Dedicated to

The Right Reverend Barbara Clementine Harris

Bishop
Leader
Sister
Prophetic Voice
Queen
Icon
Singer
Voice of justice
Friend

To Kathy, my wife and Mark Anthony, our son.

To the children of the Diocese of Massachusetts and to
Ulrike Guthrie, whose careful attention gave life to this story.

Special thanks to Tracy Sukraw, editor of *The Episcopal Times*
for supplying important information for this work.

The primary events of this book are true, but the childhood events are fictionalized versions of real events.

"As you grow up in the church, I am sure you will learn the Apostles' and the Nicene Creeds. If you are not ready yet to read or say the entire creed, you can learn and remember this little verse that I was taught in Sunday school. It is called The Children's Creed and it also tells what we believe about God.

I believe in God above,
I believe in Jesus' love,
I believe the Spirit too,
Comes to teach me what to do.

I love you and I pray that God will bless you in every way."

– Bishop Barbara Clementine Harris from a letter
   to the children of the Diocese of Massachusetts, May 2000

"We cannot—and we must not—overlook the fact that this woman who is being consecrated today is not just an American woman. She is a black woman. So I would say, as of today, that the camel has gotten through the eye of the needle."

– The Reverend Paul M. Washington, Rector Emeritus,
   the Church of the Advocate, Philadelphia from his homily
   at Bishop Harris's ordination, February 11, 1989

"Sitting around that campfire, some kid is going to say, 'So who is this Barbara C. Harris?' And there will be a counselor there. And that counselor will say, let me tell you the story. Let me tell you about this girl who grew up in Philadelphia. . . .The counselor will tell a story of a woman who offered herself. . .just in little steps, in the pattern of Jesus Christ.

What you are, Barbara, is an icon for us. You are an icon for us— somebody we can look at and see that power. We can see that power of Jesus Christ in you."

– Bishop M. Thomas Shaw, Bishop of Massachusetts,
   February 13, 1999

TABLE OF CONTENTS

Imagine if you will, a girl named Anna. It is her birthday, and she is terribly excited. She wakes up early, gets out of bed without her mother calling her, and gives her mother no trouble about getting ready for church. This is a very special Sunday; the rector told the whole parish that the bishop is coming to their church, and Anna is very happy about this.

Many people come to church this Sunday. Anna is particularly glad that she and her mother have come early because the little church is soon packed. Everything looks bright and more beautiful than usual. The choir sings all the songs Anna loves and the verger, who typically looks sad, is smiling today. An abundance of flowers decorate the church, and the candles seem to burn more brightly than ever before.

Anna loves the bishop. The bishop tells several funny stories and reminds the parish that Jesus loves everybody. People are confirmed, baptized, and received into the church. Suddenly Anna hears her name. The bishop is calling her. Anna's mother has told the bishop that it is Anna's birthday, and the bishop calls her up for a special blessing.

Three years later the rector again announces that the bishop will be visiting soon. Again she is all excited. Again she goes to church early and sits up front. As the congregation sings, she closes her eyes and waits for the bishop to arrive in the chancel. But when Anna opens her eyes she is startled to see a man where the bishop should be. He does not sound like the bishop, does not talk like her, and quite definitely does not look like her. "Mom," Anna says, "that can't be the bishop. Why is he acting like a bishop? A bishop is a beautiful black woman."

Anna had met Bishop Barbara Harris and in her eyes, a bishop must be a woman. A beautiful black woman.

ONE

Quaker State: Philadelphia

"Hey, you! Black girl!"

Barbara kept walking and did not turn around.

"What are you doing on my block?" the voice demanded.

She knew the voice belonged to a white girl. Barbara walked by the girl's house almost every day, and heard her playing with her friends regularly. Even though Barbara's mother always told her to be polite to strangers, Barbara had never spoken to the girl. She had figured that silence was a form of politeness. If she said nothing and they said nothing that was fair enough.

Barbara kept walking. All she wanted was to finish her errand for her mother and get back home to play with her sister. "Why do things like this happen when I'm in a hurry?" she silently asked to herself. "Whenever I want to get something done, and done quickly, somebody or something gets in the way."

"Black girl! This is Philadelphia, and I am asking you, *what* are you doing on my block?"

Finally, Barbara turned to face the voice yelling at her. She was right. It was the white girl who lived a few blocks away from her own house. The girl was older and a lot bigger than Barbara. The girl's size did not scare her. Everybody always told Barbara she was skinny, but she was comfortable with herself. Barbara looked straight into the girl's eyes, up and down, turned around, and started walking.

"Don't you hear me talking to you?" the girl shouted.

Barbara could hear the sound of rapid footsteps behind her. The girl was running after her.

Since the moment the girl had first spoken, Barbara instinctively began searching for a way to protect herself. There were stones on the sidewalk, and Barbara knew what she needed to do. She bent down and picked up a brick, feeling its weight in her hand.

Spinning around, Barbara's eyes flashed. In her calmest voice she said, "Don't mess with me, you hear? Just leave me alone." She heard herself saying the same thing three times. Each time, her voice got louder, but she was calm.

The girl stopped in her tracks, mouth open, and eyes wide. Barbara started towards her. But before Barbara could take five steps, the girl turned around and ran away.

A few weeks after that, the girl started to wave to Barbara whenever she walked past. Barbara just said, 'Hi,' and kept on going.

Barbara Clementine Harris was born to Beatrice and Walter Harris on June 12, 1930, in Germantown, Pennsylvania. The Harris family was what are called *cradle* Episcopalians, which means their family has belonged to the Episcopal Church for many generations. Beatrice Harris, known to her friends as Bea or Ms. Bea, had worshiped for many years at the Parish of St. Barnabas.

Episcopalians take pride in knowing the traditions of their church and the liturgical events and saint's days that occur every year. For example, most Episcopalians know that the church year begins in early December, a time called Advent. This is a season when the church prepares to celebrate the birth of Jesus. Advent leads to Christmas, Christmas to Epiphany, Epiphany to Lent, Lent to Easter, Easter to Pentecost, and so on. In addition, Episcopalians know the important feast days or saint's days. John the Baptist, the feast of St. Peter, and the conversion of Paul are celebrated by nearly every Episcopal parish in the world. There are also the local feast days that celebrate the patron saints of individual parishes. St. Barnabas is the unofficial patron saint of Germantown—at least for local Episcopalians.

Ms. Bea's family figured that their second child would be born in June. The month of June had many important feast days, and the family was hoping that June 11, the feast of St. Barnabas, or June 24, the feast of John the Baptist, would be the day of the baby's birth.

John the Baptist was a cousin of Jesus and the gospels portray him as the man who paved the way for the ministry of Jesus. John fearlessly proclaimed a ministry of conversion, baptized Jesus, and was beheaded for speaking the truth.

Not much is known of Barnabas, the man early Christians called the "son of consolation." He sold his possessions and gave the money to the apostles to support their ministry. Later they assigned him to work with Paul, who was an apostle to the Gentiles—the non-Jewish believers. Obviously, Barnabas was a tremendous help to Paul, who suffered greatly at the hands of those who opposed the message of Jesus.

As well-informed Episcopalians, the Harris family was excited that their child's birth would be close to one of these important religious celebrations. Truth be told, Ms. Bea was less concerned about the date her child would be born, than she was about having a relatively painless delivery. Most of all, she prayed for a healthy baby.

The family awaited the birth of their second child with great joy. Whenever Ms. Bea felt the child moving inside her womb, she would laugh. Sometimes the child gave a swift, hard kick and this led many to believe that the baby was a boy.

In those days before ultra-sound, there was no way to learn the gender of a baby before its birth. But this did not stop people from guessing or hoping, and the Harris family was no exception. Joey, the Harris's first child, was thrilled that she would finally have a baby brother. It was an exciting time in the Harris house as the month of June began.

As it became increasingly obvious that Ms. Bea would be delivering the baby in early June, the family decided to name the child Barnabas. Walter Harris was sure his second child would be a boy. And the more he thought about it, the more he realized he wanted a son who would be like St. Barnabas—brave, dependable, and able to bring consolation to others.

But what no one knew was that the child they we so sure was a boy was, in fact, a girl. In many ways, this indicated some of what this new child's future held. Later, family members and friends would say, "You can never tell what Barbara might do."

At the beginning of the twentieth century, most babies were born at home, with the help of a midwife. Ms. Bea's mother had delivered many babies, and she was ready to deliver her grandson. On June 12th, when it became clear that the birth of the child was near, everything was made ready. Water was boiled, new sheets were spread, clean towels set out, and soap, scissors, and a pot on the stove were all ready.

Ms. Bea's labor pains increased. It was going to be a hard birth. Her family stood around her encouraging her and wiping the sweat from her forehead. They urged her to push. Just when she thought she could bear it no longer, out came the baby, and Ms. Bea heard the clear cry of her newborn child.

"It's a girl!" the family shouted. The baby's cry was kind of funny. It sounded like regular crying mixed with happiness. At first, Walter was a little disappointed that his second child was not a son, but soon he was swept up in celebrating the life of the new child.

And so Barbara was born twelve days before the feast of John the Baptist, celebrated on June 24th, and one day after Barnabas, June 11th.

"If she had been born yesterday, we would have named her Barnabas," Ms. Bea said.

"Apparently, she doesn't like the name Barnabas," her father said, laughing.

"Oh, you are beautiful," Ms. Bea said, kissing her daughter. She turned to her husband and handed him the baby. "I know you wanted a boy, but there is still time."

"Don't worry. I'm so happy that you're doing all right and that this sweet thing is okay."

"Oh yes, it was a tough delivery. This girl will be a fighter, I can tell."

"Just like her mother," her father said. "May God bless this fighter and all our family."

Walter Harris kissed the child, kissed his wife, and presented the newborn to her sister Joey.

"My own sister," said Joey. "And she is not a boy."

"Your sister, Barbara," her mother said.

"I like that name," Joey said. "I like that name."

Eleven years later Walter and Ms. Bea would have a son, Thomas Harris, named after his maternal grandfather.

■————■

Every year on June 11, the Church of St. Barnabas—the parish where the Harris family worshiped— commemorated the life of Barnabas. Festivities began with Holy Eucharist, after which the parishioners gathered for a potluck meal. It was a great time—a time of celebration and fun for the people in both the parish and town. Some of Barbara's lifelong friends later said that it was all that celebrating that destined her to bring so much joy to the church. . .but we're jumping ahead of our story.

On the Sunday closest to June 11th the rector would preach on the virtues of imitating Barnabas. Often the rector described Barnabas's journeys with Paul. These two traveled all over the ancient world, with Barnabas encouraging Paul when things got difficult. The rector pointed out similarities Barnabas shared with members of the parish; challenging those listening to him to be like Barnabas, maintaining a cheerful and determined spirit in life.

The Black community in Germantown experienced many trials and challenges. Unemployment and discrimination affected many families. The rector constantly reminded them to never grow weary. St. Barnabas's strong, stony structure embodied hope and strength to weather the storm. For those who attended, church was a morale booster. Their faith made a difference in their lives. Barnabas stood as a symbol of the people's religious values, their friendships, and their faith.

It was into this community of faith that Barbara was born. She would soon grow to value, appreciate, and carry on the faith that was alive at St. Barnabas.

As proud Episcopalians, members of the Harris family were happy to live close to the church—a church that was respected and loved in the neighborhood. The church was like a second home to the Harrises.

Perhaps it is no surprise that Barbara comes from a place like Pennsylvania. From the start, she had history on her side. Early Pennsylvanians fought for independence, advocated for the oppressed, and respected the rights of the American Indians. Pennsylvania's anti-slavery campaigning came from its Quaker roots. Looking into history, Pennsylvania seems just the right place for Barbara.

Pennsylvania means "Penn's woodland" and is named for Admiral Sir William Penn, whose son, William Penn, founded the colony in 1682. In spite of his high social position and excellent education, young William shocked his upper-class associates by embracing the beliefs of the Society of Friends—the Quakers—which at the time was illegal in England. He used his inherited wealth and rank to benefit and protect his fellow believers from persecution.

George Fox, the son of a Leicestershire weaver, is credited with founding the Society of Friends around 1650. The Society's members rejected rituals and oaths, opposed war, and soon attracted considerable attention—mostly hostile.

Despite the unpopularity of his religion, Penn was socially acceptable in the King's court because the Duke of York—who later became King James II—trusted him. At that time, the Duke of York was Anglican; but later he would convert to Catholicism. Who knows? Perhaps his courage to convert came from his relationship with Penn. King Charles I had two sons, Charles II and James. James eventually succeed Charles II as king for just a few years; before he was exiled for his faith. King Charles II—James's brother—owed William Penn a large sum of money from a loan made by Penn's father.

Penn asked King Charles II to grant him land in the territory between Lord Baltimore's colony of Maryland and the Duke of York's colony of New York as a haven in the "New World" for the Quakers as payment for the loan. With the support from James, the Duke of York, Penn's petition was granted. King Charles II signed the Charter of Pennsylvania on March 4, 1681, and officially proclaimed it on April 2. The King named the new colony in honor of William Penn's father.

The Commonwealth of Pennsylvania, a mid-Atlantic state, and one of the thirteen original colonies that became the United States, has a most interesting history, and many noteworthy citizens throughout history.

Pennsylvania's citizens pride themselves on the state's early contributions to America's greatness. And rightly so. William Penn believed in the power of the human spirit, treating people with respect and giving each person a place in society. He founded the state on egalitarian principles for peoples of all religions. Benjamin Franklin, a son of the state, was one of the signers of the Declaration of Independence, and he helped mold the Constitution.

Many Quakers were Irish and Welsh, and settled in the area immediately outside of Philadelphia. French Huguenot and Jewish settlers, together with Dutch, Swedes, and other groups, contributed smaller numbers to the development of colonial Pennsylvania. The mixture of various national groups in the colony helped to create its broad-minded tolerance and cosmopolitan outlook.

Religious tolerance was one of Penn's most important legacies. From the start everyone had religious freedom. At the time, English Quakers were the dominant population, although many English settlers were Anglican. The English settled heavily in the south-eastern counties, which soon lost their frontier characteristics and became the center of a thriving agricultural and commercial society. Philadelphia became the metropolis of the British colonies and a hub of intellectual life.

For our story about Barbara, another important aspect of Penn's legacy is the Quaker opposition to slavery. Some 4,000 slaves were brought to Pennsylvania by 1730; most of them owned by English, Welsh, Scottish and Irish colonists. The census of 1790 showed the number of slaves had increased to nearly 10,000, and about 6,300 of them had received their freedom. It is noteworthy that the Pennsylvania Gradual Emancipation Act of 1780 was the first emancipation statute in the United States.

As a result of the Gradual Emancipation Act, the slave population had dropped to 64 by 1840, and by 1850 all of Pennsylvania's slaves were free unless they were fugitives from the South. The Black community had 6,500 free people in 1790, growing to 57,000 by 1860. Philadelphia was their population and cultural center.

What does all this history have to do with our story? Barbara's great-grandmother was a slave, who had moved to Philadelphia. "I can tell you things that I have seen with my own eyes, that you would not believe," she would sometimes say to the family as they gathered in the evenings.

"Tell us something that you saw."

Depending on her mood, she launched into a story of how the slaves plotted their escape, how the owners punished them when they were caught, and how every slave desired to have a better life. Those listening to her would sometimes burst into tears, and she would look at them, full of compassion, and say softly, "Thank God, we have come over now. Things are a lot better now."

No one can guess how much influence growing up in a household rich in story and tradition has on the imagination of a child. This was Barbara's legacy; she spent many nights listening to stories about slaves, the emancipation, the struggles of Black people to vote and the ongoing struggle for equality. One of the messages always implicit was that she was just as good as anybody else and that *any* kind of oppression was wrong. Few of us grow up with such strong early teachings about the importance of living lives dedicated to treating each person as a child of God.

Growing up in Pennsylvania, Barbara soon learned that things were not always as they seemed. "The City of Brotherly Love" could be a harsh place to live sometimes. She had a loving and supportive family who taught her Black history and told her the dangers being faced by Blacks in the North and the South. She listened closely to these stories. One particular story she remembered was that of Absalom Jones. Interestingly, her life would, in some ways, parallel his own.

Absalom Jones was born a slave in 1746 in southern Delaware. From early childhood he worked in the "big house" as a house servant, which gave him greater opportunities to learn how to read and to learn about white society. Watching the white people in the house read constantly, Absalom would sneak peaks at their books and papers. Though he could not read, he was fascinated by the print and sometimes would spend his free time looking at the cover and pages of the books.

7

With money saved from the master, young Absalom bought an English primer, a spelling book, and a New Testament, all before he could decipher a word in them. He felt proud to possess books and made a pledge to learn to read and teach others. Begging lessons, he learned how to read, and at the age of 30, went to night school, and acquired an elementary school education. At 38, using money he scraped together by every possible means, Absalom Jones bought his freedom.

Jones, a spiritual man and regular churchgoer, moved to Philadelphia and joined St. George's Methodist Church. By then he had read most of the New Testament. He strongly identified with the sufferings of Jesus and this gave him great encouragement. If Jesus the Son of God had suffered so much, why should he not have to suffer too? Christianity appealed to him because he realized it was the religious people who were most opposed to Jesus, and despite this Jesus kept trying to make the world a better place. He thought he could live like Jesus.

Absalom Jones was an enthusiast for the Methodist Church, eventually becoming one of the first Black Sunday school teachers in the country. The church's membership included both Blacks and whites; the Blacks sitting in a designated section in the back of the church. If there were few white members on a particular Sunday, the Black members could sit wherever they chose. However, when the numbers of Black members began to grow, the clergy and the white members ordered the Black members to sit only in the balcony during the service. With encouragement from Absalom Jones, the Black members took their place in the balcony, and though some members left, the number of Black worshipers continued to increase.

Matters took a decided turn in 1787 when the white members of St. George's Church demanded that all the Black members leave. They insisted that their very presence brought about "dissention, disorder and vulgarity." With this latest and gravest insult, Jones and all the Black members walked out of church. To the amusement of some of the white members, they imitated the gospels, and they dusted the dirt from their feet and they left.

After leaving the Methodist Church, these ejected church members formed the Free African Society, with Jones as their leader. Jones met with the Episcopal bishop of Philadelphia, William White, who later agreed to accept the Black members as an Episcopal parish. Jones initially began to serve the church as a lay reader and, after a period of study, became ordained as deacon in 1795 and priest in 1802, going on to become the first rector of St.

Thomas Episcopal Church, affiliated with the Episcopal Diocese of Pennsylvania. He made history as the first ordained Black man in the United States.[1]

Jones never forgot his history. With his knowledge of scripture he preached earnestly, denouncing slavery, discrimination, and other forms of oppression. A common call in all his preaching was a warning "to the oppressors to abolish slavery."

Such events did not go by unnoticed in the Harris family who prized information and knowledge. That is why they would spend so much time talking about history and listening to one another. Indeed, Barbara heard many stories about Pennsylvania, slavery, and the church. At times, it seemed as if she did not pay them much attention, but they were never far from her thoughts. Her church was all Black and though the neighborhood was integrated there was an obvious division along color lines.

Later, this little girl from Germantown, Pennsylvania would build her life around working for justice inside and outside the church. In later years she would say, "I feel strongly about these issues, because I love the church and I love people. If I didn't love the church, I would not be active." Like Absalom Jones, she would stay in the church and fight for justice.

So whenever Barbara walked through the streets of Germantown, she held her head high. She knew her family loved her and she loved them. She knew her church would always be there for her. More than anything else, she knew she was just as good as anybody else. So whenever she passed the girl who asked her about what she was doing on the block, she made it her decision whether she should wave back to her or ignore her, and did not let the other girl call the shots.

"Always remember that you are somebody. There is nothing you cannot do and be if you trust God and put your mind to it," her mother told her.

Her mother often repeated this to her and her siblings. Barbara soon understood that her mother was not telling them this repeatedly because they had forgotten it but so that they would never forget it.

Barbara never forgot her mother's words; she held onto them, believing them, and sharing this belief with others.

9

---

1 This section on Absalom Jones relies on a sermon by The Rev. Phillip Dana Wilson at the Church of the Redeemer, Morristown, New Jersey, February 14, 1999 (used with permission).

TWO

"I'm Not a Boy": Family Life

Barbara loved to eat.

"Girl, you eat like a horse and never get fat," a friend of hers once said.

"It's the genes," Barbara replied. She smiled as she remembered that as a child in her house, food was always an important aspect of family life. It was in the kitchen that most memorable words were spoken.

All the Harris women love to cook and bake. Ever so often, Ms. Bea or Muz, Barbara's grandmother, surprised the family with a special treat before they went to bed. One day, coming in from the kitchen, Ms. Bea was carrying a tray with a loaf of spoon bread, her husband's favorite dessert. Joey ran towards her mother, partly to help her; partly because loved spoon bread.

"You can help feed your sister," Ms. Bea said to her daughter, with a twinkle in her eye.

And all the family watched as Josephine took a slice of the cake toward little Barbara. As soon as Josephine was in reach, Barbara reached out and grabbed the plate. Soon she had a fistful of the bread in her mouth. They all laughed.

"It seems as if the fruit did not fall far from the tree," Barbara's uncle said.

"Mom, she's finished the portion already," Joey said.

"So have I," Barbara's father replied, and as he got up to go for another portion, Barbara started crying. She wanted some more too.

"No more for you," her mother said.

Barbara put her head back and wailed.

"Let her cry," her mother said, "that's okay. But she is still not getting anymore."

In the Harris household the children could always express their views, but they would not always get what they desired.

"Oh yes, that is a good lesson," the grandmother said. "You can't always get what you want."

Even if they didn't always get their way, children still seemed to love the company of their parents and other adults. Adults fascinate children because of the stories they tell about their life experiences, stories that teach them what to expect, what the limits are, and how to have courage in life. Barbara grew up in a household that had many adults—a great-grandmother, a paternal grandmother, maternal grandparents and an uncle. This meant that there was always an elder to run to, always an arm to be embraced by, and, what Barbara loved the most, always a story to hear. There was no television at the time and so most people would gather after the day's work to talk. If the conversation was suitable for children to overhear, Barbara's parents allowed her and her sister to listen.

Sometimes the story was for pure entertainment, but oftentimes there was a message in the stories she heard, messages such as, "You must never feel that you are less than anyone else. You are somebody." She remembered this all through her life, particularly the more she heard about the suffering of Blacks throughout the United States. And she remembered it in the moments when she herself was discriminated against.

Many times she heard stories about discrimination in the south and all the ugly things that were happening to Blacks under the *Jim Crow* laws. These were laws that kept the Blacks apart from the whites. Blacks and whites were not allowed to live in the same neighborhoods, not allowed to attend the same schools and churches, and not allowed to use the same bathrooms, restaurants, and public spaces as whites. Blacks had to sit in separate sections of the buses and trains. Some town laws even insisted a Black man had to call a white man sir.

Barbara's dad became furious whenever he heard about the suffering of Black people in the South under the *Jim Crow* laws. She could see his face tighten and his eyes widen. Neighborhoods where Black people lived were always poorer and more run down.

At times the stories scared her and she found them hard to believe, because life in Germantown seemed so different. Jews, Italians, and Blacks lived together in relative harmony, though there were moments when the children would say unpleasant things to each other. Her parents insisted that no matter what she should be courteous to all people and be respectful all the time. Barbara listened carefully to her parents, but made up her mind early that she would not always be nice to people if they were unkind to her. At least she would control her tongue, but she was not going to say "Yes, sir" and "Yes, ma'am" to someone who was being rude to her.

At such times that Barbara learned much about communicating. "Don't you hear your uncle talking?" her parents would remind her, and Barbara would quickly apologize and then await the appropriate time to reenter the conversation—something she found particularly hard as she oftentimes felt that her questions were so important that she simply had to ask them the minute she thought of them. But she soon learned how to hold onto her questions. Nonetheless there were times she would say whatever came to her mind. Her mother would roll her eyes and remind her, "Young lady, you should not say everything you think of. Silence is golden. Remember that."

As she grew older, Barbara learned better to gauge when was the best time to ask an adult a question. One day she sat next to her great-grandmother, Ida Sembly, watching the sunlight paint leaves silver, and watching the leaves nod as a gentle wind brushed them. She held back for a few minutes and then she asked her a question.

"Mom Sem, do we know any famous people?" Barbara asked, looking at her great-grandmother. Mom Sem, her eyes shut, seemed to let hours go by before responding, but Barbara was not afraid of waiting.

"Do you know who General Ulysses Grant is?" her grandmother asked, her eyes twinkling.

Barbara knew that if any adult in her family answered a question with a question, you had to get the answer right or you would be told to go and look it up. Barbara knew the answer to this one.

"General Ulysses Grant was a famous Civil War general and he was also the eighteenth President of the United States," Barbara said.

"You are right," Mom Sem responded. "Now do you know that your great-grandmother met him while he was general?"

"Really?" Barbara said, her eyes widening with excitement. "Tell me about it."

"Well, one day a long time ago, when I was out working in the fields as a young girl, a group of horsemen rode up to me. One look at them and I knew they were soldiers. I also knew who the captain was. I wasn't afraid, but I did stop what I was doing to look at them."

"Then what happened?" Barbara asked.

13

" General Grant got down from his horse and asked me for a drink of water. I went to the well, without taking my eyes off him, and got him some water. He looked at it, lifted it close to his mouth then threw it away. I said to him, 'You don't have to throw it away, it's clean!' He and all the soldiers started laughing. Only I wasn't laughing. Pumping water was not easy. Then he said to me, 'People are trying to kill me, so I have to be careful. I know the water is clean, but I have developed the habit of throwing out the first drink of water. May I have some more?' I looked at him for a long time. I felt sorry for him. So I took the cup and got him a second drink. He took it and said thanks, patting me on the head and rubbing my hair. I have always kept my hair short like a boy and have always hated people patting my head.

He said to me, 'Aren't you glad, young boy, that I and so many of my men are fighting for you?' I just looked at him and said, 'With all respect, sir, I can fight for myself. And the second thing, I'm not a boy.'"

Barbara wanted to laugh, but was not sure if she should laugh in the middle of the story. So when her great-grandmother flung her head back and bellowed out a laugh, Barbara needed no other clue. Both of them laughed for a long time, and then Barbara wanted to hear more.

"You mean, you weren't afraid? One Black girl surrounded by those powerful men?"

"The women in our family are not afraid," Mom Sem replied. "And I could see you standing up to those men, too. You are very much like me."

Immediately after telling the story, her great-grandmother closed her eyes. Barbara watched her for a few moments, thinking to herself, "Could I have stood up to all those men and been unafraid?"

As if knowing what her great-grandchild was thinking, she replied, "You could have, my child. And you will."

Barbara never forgot her great-grandmother. In her later years when she started to read about the lives of influential Black women, she always kept her great-grandmother in mind as a role model. Her great-grandmother never had the fame of General Grant, she thought, but for me, she will always be a very important woman.

Barbara learned a lot from her elders about Black history. They always told her that she had nothing to be ashamed of as a Black person. Barbara knew from early in her life that she was a descendant of slaves and she never forgot that. Her parents told her that since many Blacks worked to gain their freedom showed that the human spirit could achieve anything with dedication. Her parents always insisted that she remember her history and that part of that remembering meant caring for other people, being punctual, honest, and living a good life.

But it was not only the actual conversations that engaged Barbara; she also simply enjoyed being close to her parents, particularly her father. Onto his lap or into his chair she'd squeeze herself. When her mother decided it was time for her to go to bed, she'd say so. Like any regular child, Barbara would feign not having heard and wait until her father gave her the nudge. If left up to her, she would have stayed up all night with the adults, but her mother insisted that she get enough rest.

Personally, life was quite peaceful and, for the most part, uneventful for Barbara during her childhood. Many of the serious events that the adults spoke about occurred elsewhere. Her father told many stories about events in the South, because he'd learn of those things at work from the other men. Black people were having a terrible time, according to what many of the adults said, and that troubled Barbara deeply.

Though spared much of the harsher tragedy of segregation, people in Germantown were well aware of the sufferings of so many throughout the country, especially of those in the South. Blacks were being lynched, beaten, and discriminated against. Many movements were being formed to improve the situation of Blacks throughout the United States. One such movement was the Universal Negro Improvement Association with its leader Marcus Garvey, a Black nationalist from Jamaica. He talked about building an independent Black nation in Africa. He urged Black people to stop trying to act like whites, and to take pride in their history. "The descendants of Africa should be proud of Africa," he proclaimed.

15

During the 1930s, when Barbara was a child, the effects of the Depression were everywhere. Nobody had much money, and many people had lost their jobs. Although the government tried to provide basic nutrition, people still had difficulty finding jobs to provide for their families.

The Great Depression of the 1930s was caused by the crash of the stock markets in 1929 and by the consequent slowdown of the economic markets throughout the world. People lined up on street corners to get bread, and they lined up for days to get work. Doctors and lawyers were willing to work as field hands in order to feed their families.

Many people traveled for miles and days to find work with little success. It was a common sight in those years to see men and women walking the roads begging for food, but unfortunately most people did not have enough for themselves, never mind enough to share.

The Harris family had no more money than others at this time, but if someone came looking for a meal they would share what they had. Mrs. Harris always made sure her neighbors had food, and if they did not, she would share with them what she had. When Barbara was older, her mother recounted to her that they did well during those days because they found ways to support each other. All the adults worked in order to ensure that the children had what they needed.

In later years, Barbara remembered hearing stories of how she was born when the Great Depression started and also remembered how everything back then was mended, fixed, and used again. It was a time when even children joined the long lines to get bread.

"Why isn't there enough food for everyone?" Barbara asked.

"Because many farms have had bad crops, people have lost their jobs, many do not have much money, and some people are being very selfish," her mother said.

"If I had enough money I would buy food for everyone."

"I'm sure you would. But for the time being we just have to be patient. I am sure things will get better; they always will."

"How do you know that?"

"The longer you live, the more you trust that God will provide. Don't worry, we have all been through more difficult times than these. So, what did I say?"

"Things will get better; they always will."

It was never the case that the Harris household was wasteful, but they were now more attentive than ever to the things they had. Nothing was ever thrown out. On the rare occasions there was left-over food, it was used to make soup for the next few days. Socks, shirts, and pants were constantly being patched and mended to help extend their usefulness. Old clothes were taken apart at the seams and resewn to fit other purposes, usually by Barbara's grandmother who was a great seamstress and made beautiful recycled clothes.

One of the things that Barbara never forgot was how these difficult days helped form her sense of generosity and her work ethic. Work took on a new meaning during the Great Depression. Everybody who could work, worked. Barbara developed a love-hate relationship with work. She knew it was important, but she did not always like working when others told her to work nor did she always want to do the work they insisted that she do. Some days, she preferred being with her friends, playing, or reading a book rather than doing house chores.

The men in the Harris family found employment by doing odd jobs. They were good with their hands and there was always something in need of repair. Some days they had more luck than others finding work, because everybody was looking for something to do back then so the competition was fierce.

Many of the women, who before the Depression had stayed home to take care of their homes and families, now did domestic work outside their homes, cleaning schools and the homes of wealthy people. Barbara's grandmother, for example, cleaned the local school.

Coming home from school one day, Barbara saw her mother and grandmother talking. By the look on their faces, she knew they were planning something. She guessed she was not going to like this idea.

"Good evening, Mom," she said as she hugged her mother. She did the same to her grandmother, noticing how unresponsive she was to her hug.

"Would you like to earn some pocket money by working in the school with me?" asked grandmother.

Barbara looked at her mother with a confused look that said, "Are you betraying me?" This was a moment Barbara knew well. (In her family, one was expected to know how to read a situation and respond appropriately. "Do I have to repeat myself?" asked by an adult meant that you better obey in that moment. "Where do you think you are going?" meant you should not be going where you are going.)

As her grandmother repeated the question, Barbara's mind returned to the room.

"Yes, grandma, I would really love to work with you."

"You can smile as you say that," meant you might as well be happy because this is what you have to do.

"Why must she be spoiling my life?" Barbara thought to herself. She knew they could tell what she was thinking, but she knew with more certainty that she better not say what she was thinking. Walking towards her room, she began muttering to herself.

"What was that?" a voice from behind her said.

"Nothing Ma'm, nothing grandma!"

Barbara wondered whether her grandmother liked her. She was always fixing Barbara's clothes and telling her what she should do or not. Then if Barbara started to talk, she would tell her that silence is golden. Then if she started to run, she told her to walk. When she walked, she told her to walk faster. And then Barbara's grandmother walked around with that silly hat and ugly umbrella whether it was raining or not.

17

"Oh God," Barbara said aloud, "Imagine my friends seeing me walking down the road with her. Good God. . ."

Barbara's grandmother cleaned one of the nearby schools. Walking distance, her grandmother had said, which could mean anything from one to a hundred miles.

Barbara hated the job. The classrooms seemed so big and she wondered what the boys did everyday to leave the classroom so dirty. Her job was to dust the chairs and clean the black board, for which she got fifty cents every week. Several times she tried to get out of helping but her mother would hear none of it. Her mother gave her a few pennies to keep for herself and encouraged her to save the rest. She hated the situation, but grew to accept it because it wasn't going to change for now.

Barbara had other responsibilities too. Household chores included helping with the cooking and the cleaning, but most of the chores happened on Saturdays. Every Saturday, Barbara and Josephine helped their mother with the laundry and other household tasks. It was Barbara's job to fold the clothes after Josephine had taken them off the clothesline. By the time they were done with the laundry, the small room in the back of the house smelled of detergent, lye, starch, and fresh laundry, bleached as white as snow.

One Saturday, Barbara was helping her mother with the washing. Outside, she could hear the other children playing as she gathered clothes. She could hear the birds in the trees, the dogs barking in the fields and running around in the yard. How she wished she were free to go out and play.

"I didn't know we had so many clothes."

"You wore them," her mother answered.

"Do we have to fold them today?"

"*Carpe diem!*"

"What's that?"

"It's a Latin phrase for 'Seize the day.'"

"And what does that have to do with folding clothes?"

"Well, tomorrow you will need your clothes. So don't put off till tomorrow what you can do today."

During these chores, Mrs. Harris would sing to her daughters. She sang songs her grandmother had taught her and songs from church. Sometimes a shiver went down Barbara's spine as her mother hit the notes. Barbara loved singing with her mother. She would let her mother start, then join in the singing, harmonizing beautifully. Sometimes her mother was surprised that Barbara knew the words to so many of the songs.

'Twas grace that taught my heart to fear
And grace my fears relieved
How precious did that grace appear
The hour I first believed.

One Saturday, the Harris women were doing the laundry as usual. It was the first day of summer, and all Barbara wanted to do was to run outside and play. The sun shone as brightly as a huge ball of fire. Older men and women put chairs on their porches and stayed out of the sun. On days like these in Germantown, everything slowed down. Everything and everyone resisted the sun's rays—except Barbara.

She wanted to be free to walk in the sun, to lie in the grass and look at the sun, to just look at nature, and to run. Her mother could see that she needed to go.

"Fold five more shirts and then you can go play. And remember that I don't want to have to come looking for you."

"You're too soft on that child," her grandmother said.

Barbara folded the five shirts and was out the door, before they could say toot.

That same day, her parents waited and waited for Barbara to return from playing outside. The time for dinner came and passed, and still there was no sign of Barbara. Her parents were getting worried. In those days, if a child was missing parents sometimes feared the worst. Black children disappeared quite frequently; many families had lost their loved ones to violent acts.

Mr. Harris had returned home from work. "What do you mean nobody knows where she is?" he demanded.

"She said she wanted to go out and play. That's the last I saw of her," Mrs. Harris said.

As they were about to call the neighbors and mount a search, Barbara appeared.

"Where were you, young lady?"

"We were out looking for birds' nests," she said. Her cousin kept looking down on the floor.

"We played with the butterflies and hunted for birds' nests all afternoon, then waited until the birds went to sleep," she said smiling.

"You did what, child? You know how dangerous things are these days?" her grandmother asked.

"You don't do that again," her father said. "And I don't expect to have to repeat myself."

"Yes, dad," she said, looking serious for the first time. When he went to his chair, she started to smile again.

"Mom, when we went to the park, all the white children left. So we had the park all to ourselves. It was so much fun."

Something about her smile prevented her mother from getting angry. She hugged her, "Please don't do that again. Your father and I were really worried."

"Okay, mom. I promise never to leave the house and stay out late without telling you. Sorry."

Barbara never did make that mistake again. She knew that her parents had been very scared by her absence. Never again did she disappear without informing her parents, at least not for too long. Part of what made her aware of how fortunate she was, was living where she lived and having parents like the ones she did. The children of Germantown heard many horrific stories about discrimination and the effects of the Great Depression on children elsewhere.

Having strong parents and a church community helped remind Barbara that people had lived through far worse times. Her father sometimes would remind her that tough times produced tough people.

"What do you mean by tough people?" she asked, looking up into his eyes.

He laughed. He knew she understood him and was just joking, but he answered anyhow.

"Tough people are those people who know how to thrive in tough times."

Barbara wanted to be a "tough person." She wanted to make her parents proud and she wanted to be proud of herself in life. She started asking herself from an early age what she would do with her life, but at first she had no clear idea, apart from saying she wanted to be "tough."

Toughness for Barbara came from many surprising avenues. Part of her toughness came from the discipline of studying, doing her daily chores even when she would rather be playing, and hearing about what was happening in the United States and the world. A lot of the information about what was happening in the world she heard from her father. She could listen to him for hours on end.

On the days she did not feel tough, she remembered the story her great-grandmother told about meeting General Grant. There was no need to fear anyone but God alone. She forgot where she heard that, but it was true.

When Barbara was thirteen, her father, like many other men in the neighborhood, got a job at a steel mill. During World War II there was need for a lot of steel. Work at the mill was dangerous, but it was paid decently enough for Mr. Harris to provide for his family. Mr. Harris saw his job as very important. His experience in the military enforced his sense of order and discipline. He was always punctual and loved to boast that he was never late for a meeting. But he was a delightful man who loved to make jokes, talk to his children, and help around the house. When his son, Tom, Barbara's brother, was old enough he taught him about horses and things he had learned in the military, and when he grew up, Tom joined the military.

Mr. Harris spent time in the yard, pruning, fertilizing, and watering the various fruit trees when he was not at work. When Barbara grew older, she would sometimes follow her father around as he tended to the peach trees and mulberry bushes. Whenever she hung around her father like this, he always found something for her to do. "The devil finds work for idle hands," he would often say. Barbara liked the fact that he treated her as if she were a boy. "There is nothing a man can do that a woman can't," he said to her. Her uncles and grandfathers all said the same thing and Barbara grew up believing them.

St. Barnabas Episcopal Church was a special place in Barbara's life. She learned so much there. Every week she looked forward to hearing and reading new Bible stories. By the time she was eight, Barbara had read all the books in her parents' house and a lot of the Bible. She wrote down her favorite passages in a little book of blank pages. Sometimes, she wrote commentaries on what she had read and compared her views with those of others. The more she read the Bible, the more she saw connections between her favorite hymns and the Bible. She felt pleased about her discovery.

Oftentimes, she struggled to figure out what a passage meant. If she could not understand it she asked her parents. Then she went back to her book and rewrote the passage in her own words. "I think my views make more sense," she would often say to herself. As her love for reading developed, so did her desire to write commentaries on what she read.

Barbara realized words are powerful, they can inform, deceive, hurt, heal, and bring peace. She desired to know how to use words, both written and spoken, to her advantage. Father Thomas, the priest at the church, spoke clearly about God and she liked what he had to say. A lot of what she heard on the radio also impressed her, and she particularly loved to hear recordings of famous men as they made speeches. At times her parents would hear her making up speeches to give at imaginary events.

"That child is wise beyond her years," her grandfather loved to say.

"I don't mind," her mother said. "As long as she realizes that she is still a child. I swear sometimes she thinks she is older than I."

They all laughed.

———

School, work, and church formed Barbara's personality on a daily basis, as did her family. She loved her sister, Joey, and people always commented on how well they got along together. But like all sisters they had their ups and downs.

Like any older sister, Joey loved to remind Barbara that she was the younger sister.

"I was born first," her sister said, "and I am the best."

"That doesn't make you the best," Barbara responded.

"Then what makes somebody the best?"

"Being good or the best depends on what is in the heart and in the head."

"That may sound great, but it doesn't make any sense," Joey said making a face. "I was the first grandchild in the family."

"And I am the second," Barbara replied. "And I will have you know, we are all God's children."

"Well, I was born first and when I was born. . ."

Their mother walked in. "What are you girls arguing about?"

"Nothing, mom."

"She said that she is the first grandchild and that she is more special," Barbara said, as a tear rolled down her cheek.

Her mother reached out, and, embracing both of them, she pulled them close.

"Listen, you both belong to me and I love you both equally. We are a family and we must love each other. The world will put you down enough. In this home we have to learn to be kind to each other," Barbara's mother said, looking first at Barbara then at Joey. "Now Josephine, tell Barbara that you are sorry. And Barbara tell your sister you forgive her."

"I am sorry."

"I forgive you."

"Now hug each other and let's go eat some apple pie."

And so it was out of the hurly-burly of everyday encounters that Barbara's desire for justice and understanding was honed.

Yet her expression of that justice and understanding was just as often playful as it was serious. Once while the adults were having a conversation, Barbara was playing the piano. She stopped suddenly and walked over to the adults.

"Segregation is wrong and must never be condoned. We must get up, stand up, and speak out for our rights. And as Marcus Garvey said, 'Up you mighty race, you can accomplish what you will.'"

Her mother would roll her eyes at these grand pronouncements coming from her young child, but she also knew that once Barbara started talking there was no way to get her to stop.

"Barbara, where do hear these things?" her mother asked laughing.

"I read them in books, the newspaper. You know, I read anything I can find."

"Well, go and play with your sister, I'm tired." She patted her daughter on the head, laughing to herself. "And let your sister get in a word, please."

Off she would go to find her older sister.

"Hey, Joey, what you doing?"

"Talking to my friend, Aber."

"I don't see anybody."

"Can't you see my friend Aber Crombie? He wants to shake your hand."

For a moment Barbara was not sure if there was actually a person that she couldn't see. She had seen her sister talk to this invisible friend before, but this was the first time her sister had wanted to introduce her to him.

"I don't see anybody." Barbara said.

"Well, something must be wrong with you."

"Let me hear him talk."

"He won't talk when you're around."

"Well then, if I can't see him and he won't talk to me, you can keep your friend. I don't want to be friends with someone who doesn't want to talk to me."

Barbara walked away from her sister, who watched her to see if she would look back out of curiosity. Barbara never looked back. That was the last time Josephine tried playing tricks on Barbara.

"I like that about Barbara," Joey said to a friend one day. "I don't know how she manages to stay so cool and calm, no matter what happens."

"Yeah, she's cool. You should be glad you've such a cool sister," her friend replied. "Mine follows me around all the time, and she's older than Barbara."

"Sometimes, Barbara acts like the older one."

"That's all right. Just don't let her get too high and mighty." The two friends soon started talking and laughing about other things.

"Mrs. Harris really has a nice daughter," Mr. Brown said, as Barbara and her friend walked past his house on her way home.

"Oh, yes," his wife replied. "That is how I like to see children grow."

"Yes. Notice how she is always polite and is never rude like those other children."

"She's a real lady."

"You know the other day," he continued. "I was feeling sad about what happened to that Negro boy. Barbara came up and asked me what was wrong. I didn't want to tell her, but she insisted. Guess what she said to me?"

"What?"

"Don't I tell you not to answer a question with a question?"

"Come on, man!"

"She said, 'Mr. Brown, what those people did was wrong. But we must be strong, because our people will overcome. Good always overcomes evil.'"

Barbara was a precocious little girl. You never knew what would come out of her mouth. Many people at church thought that she was wiser than some of the adults. Even her teachers recognized something special about Barbara. She was not the brightest in the class, but there was something about the way she thought that made her very different. A lot of Barbara's ability to think on her feet and to know the appropriate responses at the right time came from her experience of listening to what the adults around her shared. While it is true that many children have adults around them all the time, what was different about Barbara was that she paid close attention to what they said and what they did not say.

On Saturdays or Sundays, when family and her parents' friends came for dinner, Barbara would do all her chores quickly so that she would have time to listen to the adults. "It sharpens my brain," she once told her mother.

Her parents and their friends talked a lot about the economy, the strange things happening in Europe, discrimination, their family, the church, and the future of America.

Barbara listened carefully. She knew that what they were saying was important. At times her mother would send her out of the room. In those moments, judging from the tone in her mother's voice and the look on her father's face, Barbara knew that no arguing would be allowed.

She looked forward to hearing the adults tell stories. Some of the stories warned the children about the dangers of life, some told them about the importance of respecting their elders and some were just funny. Barbara was always the one who insisted on hearing a story.

As soon as she got a chance she would beg, "Tell me a story." The men and women told her tales and legends about giants, men and women from the Bible, and ancient spirits. Quite frequently they told stories about escaped slaves, freedom fighters, segregation in the South, and fables from Africa. No one could predict the topic of stories. The only rule in the Harris house was to remember that the children often listened.

"You're scaring the poor children," Mrs. Harris said interrupting a story about a man with fanged teeth.

"All right," the storyteller said. "Whoever wants to leave can leave."

All the children left except Barbara.

"I knew you would stay," he said, continuing his story about the ex-slave who had come back to haunt the plantation.

Sometimes the stories were just plain funny. At those times, the Harris house rocked with laughter. Her grandfather never laughed without pounding on the table or slapping his wife on the back. She sprang out of her chair howling, which usually set off uncontrollable fits of laughter among the children. The adults laughed so hard that tears rolled down their cheeks. Those were happy times.

Barbara tried to memorize these stories and jokes. She would repeat the stories to herself until she remembered them. When she repeated the jokes to her family and friends, she added her own interpretations. She soon developed a style of telling jokes and stories that was guaranteed to leave everybody laughing.

From the start, Barbara was quite independent. It was as though being left-handed and the middle child gave her the courage to take risks.

During the holidays, when the family did not go on outings, Barbara would watch her grandmother cook. Sometimes she never left the house but would just keep her grandmother company, try to dip her finger in the batter without her noticing, and engage her grandmother in conversation.

"Muz, why is there so much suffering in the world?"

"Ah, my child, that's a good question. I think the answer is that man has turned away from God."

"What can I do?"

"Barbara, my child," her grandmother said. "Be good, always try

25

your best to be good. And if you can't be good, be careful. We are living in serious times."

"Why are the times so serious?"

"Because people don't know how to love."

"I thought it was easy to love."

"Nothing in life is easy," her grandmother said. "But I want you to know that if you try to love, you will love and if you try to be peaceful, you can be peaceful. All things are possible for those who believe in God."

"I believe you. I believe," Barbara said, reaching up to kiss her grandmother.

Before her grandmother could respond she was out the door.

"That child is a swift one," she said to Barbara's mother.

"True. People think she is a happy-go-lucky, but she is also sharp. I wonder what she will be."

The two women looked at each other, then walked towards each other. They hugged.

"You're a good mother!"

"You too, you too."

The grandmother went out to sit on the porch. There was Barbara sitting under a tree with a serious look on her face. Her grandmother got up and walked over to her.

"You know Muz, I believe you. I like the fact that there is nothing that I cannot do."

"It's true my child, it's true."

Her great-grandmother had died a few years ago, but she still felt her presence in the house. Sometimes Barbara thought she saw her. She never shared this with anyone. Quite frequently though as she went to bed, she could hear her great-grandmother's voice saying, "With all respect, sir. I can fight for myself. And the second thing, I'm not a boy."

"Wake up, Barbara! It is time to go to church." It was her father, shaking her.

THREE

"You're Black": School Life

It was a bright Philadelphia day and Barbara sat in her classroom waiting for the teacher to arrive. Rows of benches, each with a table to write on, made their way in neat rows to the teacher's table. A porcelain vase held a bright red rose, probably given by a goody-two-shoes student, Barbara thought. The teacher had arranged a neat pile of books on the desk, among them a Bible and a dictionary. As the students waited a fly buzzed into the classroom. The girls giggled and Barbara ducked as the fly flew over her head. She was about to get up and chase after it when the door opened. In walked the teacher. Barbara kept watching the fly. As the students stood up and said, "Good morning, ma'am," the fly flew through the window.

It was an integrated elementary school, which was not the norm for schools throughout the country at the time. Most schools were segregated, meaning that Black students went to one school; white students to another. But Philadelphia was progressive. Barbara had heard a lot of talk about this and it always made her look at her classmates every time she was in class. Why would people not allow Black children to study with white children? As she looked at the other students, she made a mental note of the brightest ones in the class. She ranked herself as being pretty good. She was Black and certainly one of the better students. Goes to show, she thought, anything a white student can do, she can do too.

The school bell rang. Barbara could never figure out how they had timed it so that as soon as the teacher walked in and the students said good morning, the bell would ring. It was time for prayer. The students sang, "Jesus loves the little children" and the teacher read a prayer from a book. "Children you may be seated." And as if they were all programmed to sit at the same time, they all sat.

"Today, I want to tell you about the progress women are making in the world. Shortly after World War II, many women started to work outside of the family home. Now we have women teaching at universities, we have women advising the president, we have women who are scientists. Yes, women are making great advances in our country," the teacher said.

All the girls smiled. Barbara listened intently to what the teacher was saying and a big smile appeared on her face. She looked around at the other girls. All the girls, Black and white, were smiling. As is quite common among children, the girls had invented a gesture to use when they were proud of something. They would put their hands on top of their heads and pat it three times. Barbara led them in doing this. Giggles broke out among the girls and the boys.

The teacher continued. "And there is no reason why all you young girls cannot make a great contribution to this, your great country," the teacher said. This time Barbara was the only one who continued to pat her head.

At this a boy shouted out, "Not colored girls." Barbara looked at the teacher. She could tell that the teacher was shocked by what the boy had said, but the teacher said nothing. Then Barbara turned and looked at the boy. She looked straight at him with a look that her friend later said, "looked like it could cut him in half."

There was a hush in the class. Barbara kept looking at the boy. "I will see you outside," Barbara said, loud enough for only the boy to hear.

"What did you say?" the teacher asked.

"Nothing, ma'am!" Barbara replied. She thought to herself, why ask me what I said when you did not ask him.

Barbara was distracted that morning. She did not learn much because all she could think about was how to teach that boy a lesson during the recess. Somebody had to teach him a lesson and she would.

When the bell rang for recess, Barbara watched as all the children left the classroom. She got up and headed towards the door, keeping her eyes on the boy who had offended her. She followed him out to the playground. The boy turned around and saw her. He started running and she chased him. He was a fat kid and no match for agile Barbara. She cornered him next to the fence and started punching him. She lost count of how many punches she was throwing at him, she did not even hear him calling for help, nor did she hear the cheers of the other children and the voice of the teacher trying to stop the fight.

She was still throwing punches, but they were landing in thin air. The teacher had pulled her away from the boy, and her feet were off the ground.

"Young lady, that is not how we behave at this school."

Barbara was still too angry to respond. She looked at the teacher for a moment, and continued to straighten her blouse and skirt. Later that day, the teacher told Barbara that she would no longer be on safety patrol and the music committee.

Barbara felt sad. She liked doing these activities, but she felt exuberant that she had taught that boy a lesson. She knew there was nothing that the teacher had described about the women who had done great things that she or any other girl could not do, no matter the color of their skin. Barbara never forgot this incident. It made her realize that being silent in the face of any form of discrimination was not acceptable. It is funny, she thought, the boy seemed incapable of hitting a girl, yet it did not stop him from saying something insulting about women. She had heard this before. It was a classic case of good people holding some values and ignoring others. Well, she was not going to live that way. She would prove to that boy and the whole school that she could do anything she set her mind to do.

Far away in the state of Georgia a similar incident to Barbara's happened to a boy one year older than Barbara Harris. As this young Black boy played with a white friend who lived in the same neighborhood, the parents of the white boy called him inside. The next day, the Black boy asked his friend why his parents had done that. After much cajoling, the white boy told his friend that he could no longer play with him. The name of this young Black boy was Martin Luther King, Jr. He was born on January 15, 1929, eighteen months before Barbara.

There were two lessons that her family wanted her to learn from what happened to her that day in school. The first was that if one person or group of persons is oppressed, everybody is oppressed. The second was that resolving something by fighting was the least productive way to teach a lesson. Ms. Bea found new and different ways to remind her daughter of these truths all her life.

"It is not what you do, but how you do it," her mother told her.

"You mean that fighting is always wrong?" Barbara asked.

"Yes! There are other ways of proving your point. For example, you could have said to the teacher and the boy that the boy's statement was not true. Words have a lot more power to convince than blows."

"Are you sure about that?"

"Oh yes, my child."

Barbara was not yet convinced. She would have other moments when she got into fights, but she found ways to make sure her mother never found out about them. But she never forgot what her mother said either.

━━━■

Getting up was Barbara's least favorite part about going to school. Barbara always felt that just at the moment she was most enjoying her sleep it was time to go to school. She hated getting up, but there was no way around it in her family. Her grandparents got up early, prayed and did chores around the house. On many occasions the smell of food cooking would wake her up, but for the most part it required her father shaking her several times before she got up.

Overall, Barbara enjoyed going to school. She also appreciated her parents waking her up when she saw some of the other children being spanked for coming late. When the headmistress rang the bell, which signaled the beginning of school, there were always students still trying to sneak in the classrooms.

"Morning, ma'am," gasped one student as she rushed past the teacher, barely making it before the bell finished ringing. The girl took her place panting and sweating like a boxer, Barbara thought. She smiled. Soon her smile became a giggle.

"Barbara, is something the matter?," the teacher asked.

"No, Ma'am," Barbara replied, squeezing her fingers to prevent her body from erupting in laughter. Slowly her body stopped shaking; she sighed in relief.

The teacher would bid them good morning and they would respond in similar fashion. It was a rule in those days to address your teachers as "Ma'am" and, on the rare occasion that you had a male teacher, as "Sir." Then the teacher would proceed with the lessons for the day. Usually there was only one teacher per class and this teacher taught all the subjects: mathematics, English, religious studies, home economics, social studies, history, geography and science. Time usually sped by in school for Barbara, though there were days when it seemed as if the bell would never ring for recess and lunch.

During recess times she and her girlfriends would gather and play games such as *Ring Around the Rosie, Blue bird, Farmer In The Dell,* and *Old MacDonald*. They would go around and around in circles until they were all dizzy. Then the bell would ring again and it was time to return to class. When school ended the students had to stand and wish the teacher a good evening.

And though the teacher would try and prevent them from running out of the class all at once, when the bell rang, there was no stopping them.

Walking home was one of the enjoyable parts of going to school. Barbara and her friends would walk and play, sometimes stopping to look at things in the store. Since everybody knew the children and their parents, they had to be careful not to do anything that was inappropriate because word always got to their parents. When a friend reached her home or street, the others girls would scream out, "Bye, bye, sweetie pie! See you tomorrow if you don't die." Then, laughing they waved goodbye until the next day.

When Barbara got home, she first said good evening to whichever adult was in the home, then went to her room and changed her clothes. She always inspected her clothes to make sure there were no rips or stains.

In this regard, her grandmother, according to Barbara, was on a different planet, because a speck of dust to her was a stain that was impossible to remove. She was always checking Barbara's clothes and asking her "What in God's name do you do at school?" Barbara knew the correct response was silence, or "I'll try and keep them clean the next time." After changing her clothes, she would go to the living room and read, play the piano, or ask her mother if there was something she needed her to do. If there was nothing to do, Barbara would start her homework before it got dark.

The Harris living room was quite spacious. An uncle who lived with them had removed the walls to make it larger and had refinished the floor. It was everybody's favorite room in the house. On the wall a large lithograph of a tiger in a cage hung, which Barbara loved to use to scare her brother Tom.

"If you don't behave," she said while the adults were out the room, "that tiger will come out and eat you."

This would always cause Tom to start crying. Then Barbara would laugh and then hold him, telling him she was only joking.

Although she loved to play jokes on her little brother, she adored him. She saw herself as his protector, being ten years older. Even though she was the younger sister, she assumed the role of the disciplinarian. She would be quick to tell Tom what he could and couldn't do. Everybody liked her brother Tom and he made fast friends with the Italian and Jewish boys who lived a few blocks

31

away. She taught him how to defend himself and told him if the boys in his class picked on him, he should call her.

Once Tom and his class went on a trip to Washington. As he was looking at the White House a man came up and said to his group, "You colored boys get away from here." When Tom returned home and told the family Barbara was furious. "If I had been there, I would have showed him a colored lesson."

Apart from these rare difficult moments, life went on normally in the Harris home, the men working at various jobs to provide for the family and the women cooking for the men. Their family was not different from the other families of the time. The women were the ones who kept the house and did the meals, the men went out to work. Usually all the family members were home for dinner—a wonderful time to be together as a family.

At one end of the living room was a Steinway piano. Ms. Bea would play after meals. Soon Barbara expressed an interest in learning to play. She already loved to sing and thought that she wanted to become a singer or a music teacher. Ms. Bea, who was both self-taught and had tudied with a tutor, encouraged her daughter to play the piano. When Barbara showed keen interest, the family decided to send her to piano lessons. She might be a musician after all.

By the time Barbara was ten, she knew how to travel around her neighborhood and other parts of Philadelphia. Her parents told her that it was always important to know where places are and how to get there. The older she got, the clearer her sense of direction became. She just had to go to a place once, and she would know how to get there in the future. Her mother soon came to trust her on public transportation which also made it easier for her to get to and from her music lessons.

It took Barbara an hour in a streetcar and two buses to get to her piano teacher's house. Sometimes she studied her music on the bus, sometimes she read a book, and other times she looked out the window and counted houses.

On her first trip, she was happy. As she got near her stop, she admired her fingernails. They had grown so long and she tried hard not to break them. She thought of her fingernails because she wondered if the teacher would ask her to cut them. She hoped not. She played the piano at home just fine with them. But who knew?

She knocked at the teacher's door and waited for him to respond. She could hear a piano playing. It stopped and she heard footsteps. The door opened and a handsome man smiled at her and welcomed her in.

"You must be Barbara!"

"Yes, sir!" he was holding out his hand and so Barbara extended hers.

"Barbara, we have to cut those nails," the piano teacher said. He was a church organist and knew her family very well. Before she responded, he had disappeared into a side room.

"Stretch out your arms, let me see those fingernails more closely," he said approaching her.

And before she could tell him how hard she had worked to grow them, he had clipped all ten fingernails.

"Now we can begin. I am so glad you made it to class today. Help yourself to some soda, popcorn, and cookies. I will be ready for you in an hour. Thanks for coming on time."

Before she could respond, he had swooped down, picked up two fingernails that had fallen on the carpet, and gone inside the music room to attend to other students.

One day, while waiting at the bus stop after her piano lessons, a man pulled up in a car.

"Get in, I will give you a ride home," he said.

"No. My mother says I shouldn't take rides from strangers."

"I'm no stranger, I'm a nice man."

"I don't need a ride," she said. "I'll wait until my bus comes."

"Get in the car, now."

When the man realized that Barbara would not get in the car, he parked closer to the curb and then opened the door. Just at that moment, the bus turned the corner and approached the bus stop. The bus driver realized what was happening. He stopped the bus, jumped out, and raced for the car. The man quickly got back in his car and sped away.

"You did a good thing child. You did a good thing," the driver said, going over to Barbara. "When your Ma sends you out, you don't take no ride from anyone."

Later that evening, her brother and sister asked her if she was afraid.

"You know," she said, "it's strange, I kind of felt calm. I was ready to scream and run, but I was calm. I also knew that I was not going in that car."

"You mean, you weren't scared a little bit?" her brother asked.

"You're a real doubting Thomas," she said, pausing and making a face at her brother.

Everybody laughed.

She continued, "It's hard to explain. I know God is taking care of me. He will see me through everything."

The more Barbara learned in school the more she asked questions at home. She wanted to know everything and was always asking why: Why this? Why that? Sometimes she got on her parents' nerves with all her questions. But as she explained to them once, "How am I going to learn if I don't ask questions?" It was then that her father said to her, "You know, Barbara, there are more questions than answers. And sometimes the more you find out the less you know." Barbara thought about that for a long time. A month later she told her father that she agreed.

"Agree with what?" he asked.

"With what you said."

"What are you talking about?"

"About what you said the other day."

"Barbara!"

"Well, when you said there are more questions than answers. . ."

"It's true, don't forget!"

Her father started laughing. There was no way of telling if he was teasing her or if he was serious. Either way she always enjoyed asking him questions about history. She also loved to listen to his stories about life in World War I.

Barbara liked many things about school, but the thing she loved most were summer holidays. "Who invented that?" she once asked. "Whoever did, it was a great idea. Imagine two months of being free, not having to wake up early and having all day to play." Summer was Barbara's favorite time of the year. Summer meant visits to museums, to parks, to the beach and lots of fun games with her friends.

Mister Odie lived across the street from the Harris family. He had a truck and once a year would take all the kids in the neighborhood for a summer picnic. Most of the kids loved Mister Odie because of his truck, but Barbara liked to sit with him and his father, Pop Houston, and talk about the Bible and the "good ol' days," as Pop Houston liked to describe when he was a boy.

When Barbara left for school in the morning, she always waved to Pop Houston. He would wave and tip his hat to her. This made her smile. No matter what mood she was in, saying hi to Pop Houston made her happy. Whenever she returned from school, there he was. But sometimes on her return from school he would tip his hat with one hand and hold up a hymnal in the other. This was his way of telling her that he was ready to sing later, if she wished.

Pop Houston had an old Baptist hymnbook called "Gospel Pearls."

"Oh yes, my child, this book has pearls beyond price," he said to her the first time she asked about the books he always had near him. "The Bible, my hymnbook, and my pipe, these are all the things I need."

Some summer days the sun was so hot, Barbara's mother would warn the girls against playing outside. On those days, Barbara played the piano, read a book, talked to her grandmother or went across the street to sing with Mr. Houston.

"Ready to sing my child?"

"Evening, Mr. Houston," she replied. "What shall we sing today?"

"Do I have a song to sing for you today!"

Pop Houston had a twinkle in his eyes, then a smile lit up his face. He put his pipe down and opening his arms wide, he threw back his head and wailed out in baritone:

**Were you there
When they crucified my Lord?"
Were you there
When they crucified my Lord?**

"O, O, O, O," she joined in with abandon. "Sometimes it causes me to tremble, tremble, tremble. . ."

On and on, they sang, blending their voices, blending generations, blending the sweet with the sorrowful.

"On a hill far away stood an old rugged cross. . ." Pop Houston crooned and then stopped.

"I love that one," Barbara said. "Let's sing it." And they did.

Hours would pass and people would walk by and listen to both of them singing.

"Barbara, dinner is ready. Let Pop Houston get some rest," Barbara's mother shouted.

Pop would hug her and plant a big kiss on her forehead.

"You, a good soul," Pop Houston said. "A good ol' and ancient soul."

Every singing lesson ended with a caramel candy.

"Thanks, Pop."

As she walked across the street to her home, she could hear him singing:

**Ride on, King Jesus,
No man can a-hinder me**

35

Ride on, King Jesus,
No man can a-hinder me.

Later on in life, when she was down and needed a friend, she would think back to those times with Pop and a song would come to mind and soothe her soul.

Barbara attended the Philadelphia High School for Girls, a place where girls could study without the distraction of boys. Barbara's parents wanted her to be in an environment that was competitive, but gentle at the same time.

Barbara was one of few Black girls in the school. She had had decent grades in elementary school, and her teachers had confidence that she would do well. Because there were so few Black children in the school, things got uncomfortable at times. High school children can be quite mean with each other.

"See all of them looking at us?" her friend, Dorothy, asked.

"Let them look all they want."

Barbara was not going to be stopped from studying or participating in any of the school activities. She also remembered all the lessons her mother had taught her about racism. She would not judge people because of their color and she would treat everybody with respect.

As a child, Barbara had a great memory. She learned many parts of the Bible, remembered many poems that teachers taught her, and could recite many verses from Shakespeare, as well as the hymns she learned in church.

In time, she found three close friends who were loyal, respectful, and who loved to go to church. Barbara loved to laugh and so did her best friends. They always found a way to see the happy side of life.

"Hey, Barbara. I didn't know you were a writer," one of her friends said.

"What do you mean?" asked the other friend.

"My mother showed me the paper this morning with Barbara's name in it," the first one said.

"No way," said the other.

"Oh yes, I wrote an article for it," Barbara replied.

"What? You wrote in the *Pittsburgh Courier*? Let me see!" said another friend.

"And there is your name, Barbara Clementine Harris."

"Do they pay you?" the first one wanted to know.

"Yes, three dollars every week. I go down to the newspaper company and write the article, then go home," Barbara said.

"Wow," they all said.

"You can do anything you put your mind to. But you have to put your mind to it. So let's go put our mind to some ice cream."

Someone had told Barbara that the newspaper was looking for a student to write articles about children in high school. She went for an interview and wrote an article for them. They loved it and hired her. Later, this job would provide her the opportunity to see one of her favorite people, Paul Robeson. As a young journalist, she was entitled to a press pass that allowed her to go to the concert and see this famous Black radical.

Barbara worked hard in high school; her friends and teachers expected great things of her. She wanted to make the world a better place and she prayed that God would keep giving her the grace to do that.

She was growing up fast now, and her desire was to learn more and more about life. She was amazed at how much she could learn by asking the right questions. In high school, all the students had a special liking for Barbara, but she selected with special care those whom she called her best friends, for her mother always told her that "you can tell a person by the company he keeps."

After high school in 1948, she went on to study journalism, marketing, and public relations. Barbara never forgot how much fun she had had writing for the town newspaper and wanted to pursue a writing career.

37

FOUR

"I believe in God": Church Life

Father Thomas walked to the pulpit as if the whole world were on his shoulders. The parishioners had just finished hearing Matthew 25, the story of Jesus telling the crowd that whatever they did to "the least of his brothers, they did to him."

The Gospel seemed clear enough not to require much explanation, but the people knew that Father Thomas would present a certain perspective to the Gospel that they had not thought of. And so as he walked to the pulpit and Ms. Bea played the last verse of the gradual hymn, people slowly turned their gaze toward him.

"May I speak in the name of God? Please be seated. My sisters and brothers in Christ, the word of God comes to us today laying out quite clearly how God wants us to live. We cannot forget that whatever we do to the least, we do to Christ, scripture says. Therefore, God is calling all of us to examine how we treat each other. If God is calling us to examine how we treat each other, then God is also calling America to examine how it treats its citizens."

Father Thomas paused for a moment. People kept their eyes on him like a wife watching her husband returning home. In the Episcopal Church, worship was very formal and no one spoke out of turn. It was the sermon time and they watched him; his voice and message always demanded complete attention and the people gave it willingly.

"How then can America support the lynching, segregation, and exploitation of so many, because of the color of their skin? How can the church and people of good will be quiet in the face of this oppression? God is not pleased with what is happening in our country. God is not pleased with what is happening in the South. And quite frequently God is not pleased with what is happening here in Germantown."

The people listened, many shaking their heads. They knew what he was talking about and they agreed. Many of them had experienced segregation and fear. That morning as they filed out of the church many thanked him for "preaching the Word today."

When slaves were brought to America, many of them came with their native religions and other traditions. These played important roles in their search for life and meaning in America, often giving them hope in their bleak situations.

They sang and shared stories with each other as a way to keep their spirits up and pass on their traditions. Most of their stories came from ancient religious practices, but with the passage of time they learned more about the new religion practiced by their masters: Christianity.

The slave masters faced a critical moment in their dealing with these slaves: Should they Christianize them? If so, what did the Bible teach about having slaves, and what would Christian slaves mean for slavery? Was it a contradiction in terms or was it something approved of by this religion?

For centuries during slavery, many used various passages in the Bible to justify keeping slaves. But whatever passages these people used, it was clear that the kind of slavery then and the slavery practiced in the United States were worlds apart. There is no evidence in the passages concerning slavery that the slaves were separated from family, treated cruelly or with disdain or hatred. Furthermore, as the slaves learned to read, slave masters found it increasingly difficult to explain to them why the book of Exodus shows God liberating the Israelites from slavery in Egypt. More and more, there was a noticeable disparity between Jesus' call to love each other and what happened on the plantation. Slavery was built on commerce.

And so while some slaves held on to their old systems of belief, many embraced Christianity, finding meaning in the teachings of Christ. More than anything else, many felt that this religion of their masters offered the surest hope of understanding their lives in the context of captivity.

Part of what attracted many of the slaves to the new religion was meeting individuals who professed a belief in Jesus and lived life differently. These men and women actually spoke openly about

God's desire that the slaves be treated more humanely, and ultimately be set free.

Great debates ensued in the sixteenth and seventeenth centuries about whether there was merit in baptizing the slaves. Did they have souls? Could they be saved? What did it mean to have slaves who believed in the same God as the masters? Clearly, it struck many as hypocritical to talk about belief in a God of love and freedom while maintaining that the slaves had to be in shackles, not be given freedom, and not be paid for their labor.

Baptism of slaves became one way of showing some humanity and compassion to the slaves, because at least this way they were being saved from eternal damnation. After all, the owners argued, these people were primitive and did not know the Christian God. Over time, baptized slaves learned to read the Bible. This was the beginning of the end of slavery. Educated slaves discovered that it was not God's plan that they be enslaved.

As the slaves learned about the Bible and Jesus they expressed their hopes for freedom and a better life in songs called *Spirituals*. In Christianity they found tools to orchestrate some freedoms. Once baptized, they needed to go to church and many slave owners gave the slaves a free day on Sundays.

And yet, for the slaves, Christianity was always a double-edged sword offering liberation and at the same time justification for their oppression. Consequently slaves developed what many would later call the *invisible church*, worshipping separately and often secretly from their masters; using their songs to express not only their new found faith, but also their longing for freedom and plans for escape. This was the beginning of a segregation and separation they would always have to confront in search for faith, and of a yearning for freedom from racism, prejudice, and oppression.

In spite of the oppression they suffered at the hands of their white masters, there were always some whites who spoke out against the cruelty of slavery.

With the passage of time, many Blacks formed alliances with white church members and aggressively worked against the system of slavery. Amid slavery and oppression, Blacks felt that many of the white religious leaders helped articulate a condemnation of slavery. Blacks, therefore, joined the religions of those who aided them. And in the case of some, like Absalom Jones and Richard Allen, when their presence was no longer accepted by white Christians, they left to form their own church or become part of a church community accepting of them.

41

It was the Episcopal Church that accepted Absalom Jones by agreeing to the conditions that he laid down: Absalom and his followers wanted to have their own church, have control over their local affairs, and eventually have Absalom ordained as a priest.In October 1795, eleven years after buying his freedom from slavery, Absalom Jones was ordained a deacon and in 1802 ordained a priest. All this happened in Philadelphia not far from Barbara's birthplace.

■———■

All this historical background is important because it gives us a sense of what Barbara, a Black woman and a descendant of slaves, would experience in her journey to becoming the first Black woman bishop.

Like the slaves before her, she felt supported by liberal whites, while simultaneously being rejected by those whites who did not feel she should hold such an honored position in the church.

■———■

From the founding of the United States to the 1960s, religion held tremendous influence over the attitudes of Americans. America was founded as a country where freedom of worship was given the highest value. As the country grew, religion continued to claim its space in the life and psyche of the American people.

For many, church life in the 1900s centered on regular attendance, occasional family events, regular church school and the receiving of the sacraments. Baptism and the Holy Communion were the sacraments the Episcopal Church believed were instituted by Jesus Christ. To be a member of the Protestant Episcopal Church, as the Episcopal Church was then known, one had to be baptized. Baptism was a way of claiming allegiance to Christ and the church community. Baptism, a ritual that involves the pouring of water and profession of faith, was therefore the most important sacrament. Without baptism one could not receive communion or get married in the church. To receive communion—the sacrament of sharing the bread and wine in memory of Jesus—one had to be baptized.

Many other religious denominations hold similar beliefs, but they differ over who can be baptized. Since its founding, the Episcopal Church has held that children be baptized and that the parents take full responsibility to ensure that the children grow up with a love for the faith.

When Barbara was a child, baptism was just as important as the actual birth of a child, for baptism was the birth of the child into the Christian community. What could be more important than that? Some families wanted baptism as a way to ensure that the child would be claimed by God and protected from evil. Until the last few decades, infant mortality was very high, and so insuring the salvation of the child—which many thought was done through baptism—was a high priority for Christian parents.

Baptism was the distinguishing mark that identified a person as a Christian and as an Episcopalian. Today, many people frequent a church community without feeling the need to be baptized or to become a member of the parish. This was not the case in the 1800s and early 1900s. In those days, most churches required attendance on Sundays. The Episcopal Church was no exception. Ms. Bea went because she believed that the family that prayed together stayed together and she wanted her children to grow up under the formative influence of the church. "There can be nothing better," she would say to her children, "than for all you to stay close to the church no matter what. God has been good to us and you can't go wrong in the church."

For her, church was the house of God, and was so important that whenever she was pregnant she kept going to church right up to the time of delivery—so one could say that Barbara had been to church even before she was even born. As Barbara grew up, Ms. Bea explained to her why she felt it was so important to be faithful in church attendance: "God gives us everything on good days and bad days, and the love of God never ends, so once we are alive and healthy we should praise God." This was Ms. Bea's personal piety, a piety that she had learned from her parents and wanted to pass on to her children.

Even though her husband did not go to church every Sunday and some adults sent their children to church alone, that was not how Ms. Bea wanted it. Her husband went to church on special occasions—Christmas and Easter—events he called *Blue Moon Sundays*.

For the fun of it, Ms. Bea always invited her husband to church on Sundays.

"Dear, are you coming to church today?" Barbara's mother asked her husband.

"No my love, you know I only go to church on special occasions."

"God loves you on all occasions."

"I know, but I like to make church special, that's why I only go once in a blue moon."

"You and your blue moon," she said. "Okay everybody, let's go. We must never be late for the Lord's work and worship."

The women waved goodbye to Mr. Harris and Josephine ran up to give him a hug. Off the four women would go, Mrs. Harris carrying Barbara in her arms and Josephine holding her grandmothers' hands. Ms. Bea went to church with her children, whether she was doing something in church or not. It was a common sight every Sundays to see Ms. Bea leading her family to church.

When the time came for Barbara's baptism, it was a day of celebration for the entire Harris family. Her father put on his best suit as he got ready to go to church that Sunday, an occasion in itself since he typically stayed home. "This gets classified as a special time, call it a blue moon if you want," he said.

"I just hope it doesn't rain, because the wash is still on the line from last night," his wife replied.

They laughed.

"You know I am always willing to help out the farmers. We can always use a little rain."

The family had been up early preparing the house and cooking in honor of Barbara's baptism. Family and friends were coming over, and they wanted to make sure that everything was ready to receive their friends. Preparing the two small girls for church was a full-time job, but this Sunday it required a lot more effort because of the preparations for the celebration afterwards.

For the moment they were happy to be in church with Barbara all dressed up and looking fancy, but fast asleep.

When Father Thomas asked, "What name do you give this child?", her parents answered, "Barbara Clementine Harris."

"Barbara, I baptize you in the name of the Father. . ."

Barbara made a loud gurgling noise and some of the children giggled.

"And of the Son. . ." Father Thomas continued.

Barbara giggled as water poured over her forehead. She appeared to be enjoying the ceremony.

"And of the Holy Spirit," the priest said concluding the baptism.

There were smiles on all the faces in church. Father Thomas lifted up Barbara in the direction of her family and the others present and said, "We receive this child, Barbara, into the congregation of Christ's flock, and do sign her with the sign of the cross, in token hereafter she shall not be ashamed to confess the faith."

"Ba ba ba," said Barbara, drawing more smiles from everyone.

Continuing, Father Thomas then addressed Barbara's parents:

"Keep in mind that this child needs your example of what it

means to be a child of God. Bring her up in the faith, teach her the word of God, and help her to know that God is always with her."

Mr. Harris could feel the priest's gaze on him. He did not want to look up, but he finally did. Father Thomas was smiling. As Mr. Harris then looked down into the face of Barbara he could hear the priest saying, "Remember to bring her to church every Sunday." The family laughed.

Then turning to Barbara's godparents, he said, "I want to remind you that you promise to be there for this child. It is your responsibility to see that she learns the Apostles' Creed, Lord's Prayer, Ten Commandments, and all the things a Christian should know."

When the service was over, Father Thomas invited Ms. Bea and the other members to sit in the front of the church for a special blessing that marked a woman's return to church after giving birth. In some parts of the world this was quite controversial as some felt that it made childbirth look dirty and that is was inappropriate that the priest, a man, was the only person with power to cleanse the woman—indeed, that a woman even needed cleansing after childbirth, as if it were something unclean or sinful. It is important to remember that at the time all priests were men and people were not allowed to question the customs of the church. Part of the ritual was a prayer of thanksgiving for safe delivery said by the priest as he laid his hands on the mother's head.

Nearly eleven years after her baptism, Barbara witnessed her brother's baptism and her mother receiving the same blessing after the service. Typically, the women of the baptized children had to sit together, but this Sunday her mother was the only one, and Barbara remembered how solemn the whole thing seemed. There was her mother, sitting in a reverential silence alone in the pew, her head bowed for a blessing. Barbara had no way of putting into words the legacy of faith that she had received from her mother, but at that moment she felt proud of her mother. Fleetingly, she thought how serving God could be a lonely experience. It was not that her mother was lonely, but something about her mother sitting alone dressed in white and waiting for a blessing moved her.

Sunday, sometimes called the Lord's Day, was a sacred time. Almost nothing happened on Sundays that was not related to church. For children, church attendance was mandatory. A child was not allowed to say that he or she did not feel like going to church. Most parents insisted that while the child lived under their roof they had to attend church. Even when all her children were grown, there was no question about them going to church. "Once you live under the Harris roof, you have to go to church."

When Barbara was a child, life seemed a lot simpler. People worked, went to school and went to church. With the Great Depression in full swing, people did not have money to spend on trivial things. Since travel was expenseive and cars few, people spent more time with family.

Christianity was the dominant religion, and though there were a few Jews in the community of Germantown, almost everyone else was a Christian. There were Baptist, Roman Catholic, and African Methodist Episcopal churches not too far from each other, the Harris family had been faithful Episcopalians for three generations and their family had always gone to St. Barnabas.

As Barbara grew and learned about her faith, she asked her parents about other religious beliefs. She was most fascinated by the Roman Catholics. People seemed to believe that the Roman Catholic priest had special powers and the children would some-times joke that he was the boogey-man. What fascinated Barbara the most about the Roman Catholic Church was that they always seemed to be celebrating something, or processing with a statue. Her parents would allow her to watch from the gate or venture out into the streets to watch the procession.

"Who is that man?" Barbara asked, "And why is he wearing a funny hat."

"He is a bishop," one of the onlookers responded.

"A what?"

"A bishop. A bishop is the leader of a church and he is responsible for the priests and all the people in his diocese."

Right at that moment the procession passed in front of Barbara. The man in the funny hat seemed to be waving and smiling at her. She was not sure if she wanted to wave back at him. She just watched.

When she got older she found several friends who were Catholics. Sometimes she would tease them. On one such occasion her friend told her that she had to go to Confession.

"You mean you tell the man your sins? Wow. I couldn't do that."

"Oh the teacher tells you what to say, if you can't remember the things that you did wrong."

Barbara listened as the girl explained everything about Confession. The girl told about a dark box, and a drape, and going in and not knowing if the priest was on the other side of the partition. Then suddenly the curtain was pulled back and she forgot what the teacher had told her to say. But it was a nice priest and he explained everything.

Barbara was so fascinated by the whole thing. Her friends were watching her. They could tell that she was thinking up something funny to say. They were right.

"Bless me Father, for I have sinned. I stole a banana and ate the skin."

That evening Barbara told her mother what she had learned about Confession. Her mother listened and said nothing until she was finished. Then she said, "You know Barbara, you shouldn't tease your friend. Our religion is different, and you must respect other people's religion. I know you were joking, but you must not joke about religion."

Barbara could not always refrain from teasing her friends about their religion. She liked being an Episcopalian and especially loved seeing her fellow students try to say the word Episcopalian. She felt comfortable in church and loved attending church, like her mother.

On Sundays, she had the opportunity to learn new hymns and study Bible verses. Sunday School was strict and children had to behave and listen carefully to everything the teacher said. Whenever the children gathered for Sunday School the teacher would have them stand and pray and recite the Children's Creed: *I believe in God above. I believe in Jesus' love. I believe the Spirit too, comes to teach me what to do.* The children said this every Sunday for many years and Barbara never forgot it. She said it with enthusiasm and faith, and soon it was no longer simply a prayer, but rather a treasure. It made church fun.

47

St. Barnabas, Barbara's home church, was a Black church. All the members were Black and many of them were immigrants from the Caribbean. They called themselves Anglicans and recognized that they belonged to the same family as those in the United States called Episcopalians. Though many in the Episcopal Church opposed slavery and many opposed segregation, the church had opted for a less confrontational stance towards racial issues. Instead of dealing with issues of racial harmony, the Episcopal Church tried to provide Black Episcopalians with Black priests. Father Thomas was a native of the Virgin Islands, and had been called to be the rector, following a long line of impressive Black preachers.

St. Barnabas was a beautiful church. The roof seemed to stretch up and up. Someone told Barbara once that the church was built like a boat. For the longest time she would look at everything in the church to figure out why someone would say that. She had never been on a boat, but the pictures she had seen certainly did not resemble St. Barnabas. Finally, she figured out what they meant; the church did have the shape of an upside down boat. She thought it was funny and would chuckle to herself and imagine a flood on its way when she got bored in church.

The beauty of the church was apparent not only in the boat-like structure, but in the way the windows caught the sunlight. In the course of worship, a beam of light would fall on one half of the congregation and move slowly to the other side of the church. Sometimes, the children tried to sit so that the light would fall on them. They would watch the light move all the way up to the altar as the service progressed. Other times, the children tried to dodge the light. It was a game the children played discreetly in church, because their parents would punish them if they did not pay attention.

Golden candelabras with candles burning, the smell of incense, flowers in the sanctuary, and squeaky wooden benches all provided a feast for the senses and made both visitors and members feel comfortable in the church. Father Thomas made St. Barnabas feel like home to the Black people of Germantown. They owned few things in life and were happy that this was *their* church. For Barbara, the church was like a second home, a second family, and a place where she learned many interesting things.

48

As a very young child, she always wanted to be in church.

"Mom, is it time to go to church?" Barbara asked.

"No, my love, it is only Wednesday."

"Why can't we go to church today?"

"Because there wouldn't be anybody there!"

"We would be there!"

"That's true, but we would need more people to have church."

"I think we would be enough."

As a child, Barbara never left the house for church or anything else without looking in the living room mirror. Other children seemed not to care how they looked, but not Barbara. Since her third birthday, her mother noted that Barbara took a lot of interest in how she looked physically. Every pin was in place, every button, and every ribbon. And whenever her mother laid out her church clothes, Barbara would inspect them to make sure that they were perfectly ironed.

"Barbara, come try on this dress I made for you," her grandma called out.

"Oh, Muz, it is beautiful. You are the best grandmother in the whole world. The best, best, best. . ."

"Why, thank you."

"Don't I look beautiful?" she asked her mother.

"You do my love."

"Don't I get more beautiful everyday?"

"That's true, too!" her mother said. "You are the most beautiful five year old in Germantown."

"Am I the most beautiful girl in the world?"

"It's time to go to church," her mother said. "And, that mirror is going to fall down if you don't stop looking at it."

Off the Harris family went, the adults in front and Barbara holding her sister's hand, following behind. Barbara would turn around and wave at her father.

In church, there was a lot of emphasis on what it meant to help others. Father Thomas preached on the commandment of loving one's neighbor as oneself; he preached about the realities facing Black people throughout America, he preached about slavery and what it meant to be chosen by God. He insisted that his congregation be examples of love and respect. Barbara heard this message of love, heard over and over again that Jesus wanted her to be a loving person and one who cared for the less fortunate. She never forgot the things she heard in church and they influenced her life forever.

Sometimes the adults would come by to look at Barbara imitating Father Thomas. Her parents and their friends stood in amazement as Barbara rattled off things from the homily that they had forgotten. More than amazement, they were filled with amusement, for Barbara was a real comic; she imitated the priest's every movement with an uncanny precision.

The first time they played church as children there was great confusion.

"We can't do it. We have no bread," one of the children said.

"Yes, what are we going to eat?" asked another.

Barbara thought for a while. "I know," she said, "goldfish food."

The other kids were not too happy with the idea, but they went along with it and by the time Barbara fed it to them, they were quite happy to eat it.

What Barbara heard in church, she would often repeat at home for her parents. With her friends, she brought in the lessons she heard in church or sometimes used the hymns as dialogue for her dollies.

She loved to climb the trees in her yard. One day she and a friend climbed the tallest tree in her backyard.

"This will be our tower of Babel," she told her friend.

"Tower of what?"

"Babel. Didn't you ever read about the tower people built in the Bible?" she asked. "Some men wanted to climb up to heaven."

"Is that what we're doing?"

"No, we're on God's side."

"Did you read that story in the Bible?"

"Yes, I did. Do you read the Bible?"

"No, I don't always go to church either."

"Well, our church is fun. I will come and ask your mother if you can come to church with me."

"Really? I would love that."

And sure enough, Barbara went and asked her friend's parents. A year later, her friend became an Episcopalian and started to attend St. Barnabas. It was not the last time she invited friends to church.

During the week Barbara had a rhythm of things to do. As soon as she came home from school, she would have a snack, go for a walk in the yard, and start her homework before it got too dark. Then she would have dinner, help clean up, listen to her family tell stories, practice the piano with her mom, read a little, prepare for bed, kneel next to the bed and say her prayers out loud, and finally crawl into her bed.

Oftentimes when Barbara returned home from church, she would call her sister and friends and they would play church. No one ever questioned who would be the priest. Barbara loved imitating Father Thomas. She spread her arms, rocked on her heels and preached as if Father Thomas possessed her body.

Quite often Father Thomas reminded the children of the fourth commandment, "Honor your father and your mother, that your days may be long upon the earth." He then went on to talk about this commandment as being the only one with a promise. A clear sign he said, that God meant children to be obedient. Since there was a promise, there was a punishment for not obeying: being disciplined, often meaning a spanking.

Barbara's parents were no different than other parents of that time. If a child did something wrong, the child could expect to be spanked. Mr. Harris for the most part was very gentle with his children. But there was one thing he hated: children should not lie. He told his children over and over again, "Speak the truth and speak it ever, cause it what it will. He who hides the wrong he does, does the wrong thing still." Sometimes Barbara was too afraid to tell the truth. Her father had a way of knowing that she was lying. And once she did lie to him, and sure enough he gave her a whipping. After the first time, she never lied to him again.

She had a similar lesson to learn from her mother. On one occasion, Barbara was feeling quite sassy and rebellious. Her mother had asked her to finish a chore that she was working on and Barbara mumbled something under her breath.

"What did you say young lady?"

Silence.

Then Barbara mumbled something again.

"What did you say?"

"I said, if people do not like what I am doing they can kiss my feet."

"Kiss your feet?"

"Yes, that is just what I said."

"Well, we do not talk like that in this house."

"Kiss my feet!"

Before Barbara could finish the sentence, her mother had pounced on her. Holding her by the hand, she turned her upside down and gave her a few minutes of spanking. The more Barbara screamed, the more her mother hit her. She finally stopped screaming and then her mother stopped.

"Do not pass your place, you hear me."

Barbara was silent.

"Do you hear me, or do you want more?"

"I hear you Ma'am."

Barbara never made that mistake again.

It is hard to imagine in today's society, but church was just as important as school. A lot of learning about life and society happened in church. It was the place where people learned a lot about what was happening in the community and the country. So in many ways the lessons learned at home were reinforced at church and at school.

Part of what made Sunday special for Barbara was that every Sunday after church the family gathered with friends and family. At times on the way back from church, Mrs. Harris and the girls stopped by Aunt Alice's house. Aunt Alice's house was big and she always had a lot of delicious food. Barbara loved the bread and biscuits she made.

"Barbara, leave space for dinner," her mother reminded her, because there was always a big Sunday dinner waiting for the whole family back at the house, a meal that Muz had started cooking early Sunday morning. "I have never seen a child with such a big appetite and look how skinny she is."

"Leave her alone," Aunt Alice said. "I hear she does well in school, getting straight A's. That's right. She needs food because she has a lot of power in that brain of hers."

Church celebrations of special days had great appeal for Barbara. Christmas was always a very festive time with a lot of singing and dramatic presentations about the life of Christ. Then there was Lent, a somber time when the children and adults were not allowed to eat meat on Fridays and had to attend special services.

During Lent, all the children in the parish collected money for missions. The children in the parish were asked to sell magazines and books and put the money in the mite box, a special box for donations for the poor. Barbara sold more magazines than all the other children and got a cross on a chain as a special prize.

Every Lent, all the children at St. Barnabas would watch the movie, *King of Kings*. This made Lent Barbara's favorite time in church, because she got to see Bible movies at church, which she loved. She watched them attentively, and then was able to repeat the lines from the movies afterwards.

Inspired by the movie, Barbara would dress like the Queen of Sheba, which made everybody laugh. Once the laughter stopped, she would run out into the dining room, all the children following, climb on the table and shout out, "Bring me my chariot, the gift of the Nubian King." The adults would laugh so hard, tears rolled down their cheeks. No matter how often she did it, they found it funny. It was as though the movies had reinforced a love of herself and Black people. There were so few movies with Black characters in decent roles that the image of the Nubian king stuck in Barbara's mind.

The Lenten movie even influenced how she talked about boys at school. As she and her friends joked about boys one day, she made it clear what her choice had to be like and look like.

"I like that one, in the yellow pants," one of Barbara's friends said.

"Phew, I won't talk to any boy who wears yellow pants," Barbara said.

"I notice you like the guy with the funny looking head."

"Oh yes, bring me my chariot, the gift of the Nubian King."

Both girls started giggling. They laughed so hard they fell down.

"What's so funny?" a friend asked coming up on the two girls doubled over with laughter. They explained it to her, but she did not get it. Barbara then had to explain the Lenten movie and talk a little bit about the Nubian king. By the time she was through, they were all three laughing like crazy.

Another aspect of church life that Barbara just adored was the singing. As soon as she was old enough she wanted to join the choir. Barbara loved to hear the choir sing, but most of all she loved to listen as her mother played the organ and led the church in singing old spirituals. These songs gave her a love for God, a love for life, and a great love for herself as a young Black girl. It also made her eager to learn more about the Bible.

"For God so loved the world," Father Thomas said. "That he gave His only begotten Son, that whosoever believeth in him should not perish but have everlasting life."

Later that day, she repeated the whole passage to her mother.

"Where can I find that in the Bible?" she asked her mother.

"John 3:16."

And off she ran to find the verse in the Bible for herself.

As Barbara grew older and more familiar with the Bible she realized that many of the hymns had their roots in the Bible. She paid closer attention to the songs she heard in church and the songs that she heard her mother singing everyday. Music was always a big part of her life. As far back as she can remember her mother sang to her, taught others to sing and encouraged those who thought they could not sing.

Mrs. Harris loved music, and she was always singing a hymn. When she was pregnant, she would oftentimes put her hand on her belly and sing to her child. Barbara seemed to kick whenever she liked or disliked a song. Her mother could never tell the difference, but what she did know was that Barbara could kick.

"Come on now, give me the chorus again," Mrs. Harris would say to the children at St. Barnabas, where she was the music director.

"I can't sing," one boy said.

"There is no *can't* in God's book. If a frog can sing to God, so can you."

In church, Barbara learned the lessons that all things were possible. Nowadays it's harder to imagine the impact that growing up in a church can have on the formation of a young person's life and family life. But for Barbara, church was a place of importance, it was a place where she learned about belonging. Church was a place that sparked her interest in many things. She learned about how to behave in society and how to respond to people who were difficult or mean. She learned that people cared for each other in good times and bad in the church community. She also learned a lot about organizing. The church was a society within a society and she enjoyed being a part of it.

Family life, school, church, and music lessons made up Barbara's week. Each segment of her life connected like the verses of a hymn. Her life was easily integrated and as she grew she found that she enjoyed the rhythm and the discipline that life afforded her. Sundays reminded her that it was back to school the next day and she often spent Sunday night packing and preparing for school, reading ahead in her books as a way of being ahead of the class.

The older she got, the more she understood how what she heard in church prepared her for life. Nothing was too difficult for her, because her faith assured her that she could do all things. The faith given by her family made her eternally grateful to them. She thanked them through many different stages of life for giving her the gift of faith. The church embraced her and she embraced the church. The church had given her life and she would give her life to the church.

◼

FIVE

Working Hard: Adult Life

Many people considered the 1940s a time when America entered into adulthood and took its place on the world stage as a true power. America had done the world proud in World War II. Now parade after parade welcomed home the soldiers from the war. As crowds gathered to meet them, a keen eye could tell that the Black soldiers were treated differently. At some parades they were asked to remain out of sight. America had been proud of her Black sons overseas, but segregation was still a major factor back home.

It was 1948 when Barbara graduated from high school. High school had been a great experience for her and she left it behind, filled with a gratitude for her parents' commitment to education. Early on in her life Barbara wanted to be a piano teacher, but as time went by she thought it was not what she wanted to do with her life after all.

"Still want to be a piano teacher?" her friends had asked her.

"To be honest, no!" she replied. "It takes a lot more effort and money than I am willing to put into it."

"But you are good at it," they said.

"You might think so, but I don't. I am kind of mediocre. And I have learned this in life: if your whole heart and soul aren't into something, forget it. You're going nowhere fast."

"So what are you going to do when you leave school?" one friend asked.

"Leave Barbara alone," another said, "What is any of us going to do?"

"Well, I am going to be the President of the United States of America," another girl said.

They all laughed.

After the laughter, a silence descended. It was one of those moments only great friends enjoy with each other, where they can all rest in silence and lose themselves in private thoughts. No one said a word, they looked each other in the eyes only briefly, and even that contact did not cause them to break the silence. They knew the reality of the America in which they lived. Could one of them really become President? Things were not as bad in Philadelphia as it was in the South, but they each had experienced discrimination. What surprises did life have in store for them? What would become of them? Life that had once been simple had become complex, casting a shadow over the brightness and happi-ness of their childhood. There were wars, rumors of wars, maneu-verings for political power in the presidential race, and a strange sense that things would only get worse before getting better.

If one were looking from a distance, it would be hard to discover who started walking first, but these three Black women wrapped their arms over each other's shoulders and walked as a trinity of friends. Their yoke-like embrace proclaimed a promise in silence. It was a promise that they would support and be there for each other no matter what. Silence and laughter played with each other as the three girls walked home together, one going off when she was near her home, then the other, until finally Barbara was alone. Alone with her thoughts, she entered the house, wondering what she would do with her life, wondering what would become of her.

Barbara's love of writing made her decide to attend journalism school after graduating from high school. Who knows what will become of me, she thought. But at least she knew she loved to write and was good at it. Unlike her earlier dream of becoming a singer or music teacher, this was something she loved. And so off she went to Philadelphia's Charles Morris Price School of Journalism.

One night at dinner, there was the usual talk about what was happening in the country. Politics took center stage as it did quite frequently. Almost eighteen years old, Barbara was old enough to have her say. She was a young woman now and very bright. Her parents listened with attention as she spoke about what she thought the country needed at the time. Election time did have a way of dominating the conversation. The whole nation was gripped in a fascinating web of interest in the presidential race. Never before, have we seen an election like this one, they said.

The 1948 Presidential election will always be remembered as the Great Truman Surprise. Harry Truman served as vice-president under the popular Franklin Roosevelt.

"So what's wrong with the Vice-President?" someone asked.

"They say that he feels rejected by the President," Ms. Bea replied.

"It's a little more complicated than that," said one of the men who had been visiting the family. "It looks as if Roosevelt keeps everything to his chest and does not even inform the Vice-President about sensitive military issues."

"But that cannot be right!"

"Well, Roosevelt is the president and I guess he's free to do what he wants."

As Barbara walked through the living room, she heard the visitors talking. A lot of what they were saying she had read in the newspaper and heard over the radio. She had only one question about the whole thing. It was a question that she kept to herself, but found popping up in her mind every so often: "Why did Truman take the job as Vice-President?" She never gave an answer to her own question.

57

Truman had been campaigning hard for the presidency, but people seemed to be largely ignoring him. Coming as he did after Roosevelt, people called him the lame-duck president and thought he had no chance of being elected President. All the newspaper polls showed that he was likely to lose. Polls showed that only 36% of the population would vote for him. People preferred his opponent.

Truman stood up for the rights of Blacks throughout America, guaranteeing them more civil rights. His decision to look favorably on the Blacks created huge conflicts and divisions in the Democratic Party. At their convention, many of the delegates from the South walked out, because they wanted to have no part in a party that viewed Blacks as equals.

On the campaign trail, Truman soon acquired the name, "Give 'em Hell, Harry." Because he himself thought he would lose the election, he decided to speak his mind. Thomas Dewey, his opponent, bumbled his way through the campaign trail. At one point he asked some schoolchildren if they were not grateful to have gotten the day off school because of his speech, to which a young boy retorted that it was Saturday. Truman, on the other hand, was a lot better with words. He spoke his mind and insisted on his dream that the United States of America could be a better place for all people.

Polls showed that women agreed with him. It was as though women understood the plight of Black people and somehow saw that their own rights were connected to the plight of the Blacks. As one woman said on the radio, "We get treated the same as the Blacks by our men; racism and sexism are cut from the same cloth."

Forty years later, Barbara would be caught up in a church election that involved these same politics of race and gender. How ironic that as she approached adulthood, the election of 1948 so divided America. In 1988, Barbara participated in an election that many thought that she would lose because she was Black and a woman. Like Truman leading up to the election she spoke her mind. She did not allow possible results of the election to silence her voice as she spoke out on justice and equality for all. And like Truman, to the surprise of many she was elected.

Adolescence had not been a difficult time for her. It certainly was not as complicated a time as many adolescents face today. Because there were fewer temptations and risks, parents tended to give their children more freedom. Also, living in a neighborhood where everybody knew everybody else insured ample supervision.

Barbara continued to attend church regularly and at the same time to party with her friends. Saturday nights were spent gathering together and having dinner at one of the fine restaurants in town. Over these meals, Barbara and her four girlfriends got together and talked and laughed about everything under the sun, including their boyfriends.

Barbara started to grin.

"What's so funny?," one of them asked.

"You know," Barbara said, "I must have a unique talent. If you blindfold me and put a hundred boys in the room, I will choose the worst one. I seem to have no luck with boys."

"But you are so popular!"

"True. But I guess I should only have them as friends. Once we start going out, Prince Charming suddenly starts croaking."

As usual, they all burst out laughing. Sometimes all Barbara had to do was to open her mouth and the girls would double over laughing.

Then after finishing up their meal, they headed towards a club to dance. Afterwards, on their way home, Barbara always reminded them, "Remember there is church tomorrow."

"You must be joking, " one of them said.

But they knew she was not joking. She would be up and off to church the next morning.

It was a wonderful time, a time that helped Barbara know the value and power of friendship. She and these girls had been friends for many years and the way things looked, they would be friends forever. Fifty years after their high school graduation, they all showed up for the reunion.

Those days at restaurants and clubs confirmed what many knew since the day Barbara was born: she loved to talk. Some of her friends would sometimes say that she could talk paint off a wall. She knew she loved to talk, but there was something else about her that only a few people knew. Barbara also enjoyed being alone. She could stay by herself the whole day and not mind it. It was during these times that she would think about the events of her life.

On the quiet days alone she thought about her childhood, about her days in church, about outings with her family, about her extended family, about conversations she had with friends, about boys that she liked and did not like, about things that she had done and things she wished that she had done. She thought about her life as a child and the questions she used to ask her parents, and then she would think about her school days—which invariably brought a smile to her face.

One of her favorite memories was her chance to see Paul Robeson up close and in person. Robeson was an exceptional athlete, actor, singer, cultural scholar, author, and political activist. There was not one Black person in America who did not know about Paul Robeson. He was the pride and joy of Black people and parents often pointed to him as an example for their children. At the height of his career he was the most famous Black man in America and everybody loved him. His athletic, intellectual, and acting skills caused people to love him, but he was also a political activist. He would speak out against the racism in America, often because the Blacks who came to see him were mistreated.

Born in 1898, Robeson grew up in Princeton, New Jersey. His father had escaped slavery and became a Presbyterian minister, while his mother was from a distinguished Philadelphia family. Barbara respected him greatly and the more she heard about him the more she wanted to meet him. This did not seem possible.

One day she heard that Paul Robeson was coming to Philadelphia. She wracked her brain trying to figure out how she would get to meet him. Then she remembered that the *Pittsburgh Courier* would probably be the only way she could get to see him. Barbara had been writing a special children's section, *High School Notes*, for the paper. She knew she could get a pass, and she did.

When the day finally came, all her friends and family wished they had gotten the opportunity. Barbara's father was very proud of her. In later years, he would proudly tell his friends how his daughter had met the famous Paul Robeson.

Barbara had gotten a seat near the front. She loved these moments of waiting. Something about waiting on something important to happen or to see someone famous felt so exciting to her. She was admiring the "press pass," that had gotten her in; when the announcer asked all to rise to welcome the "great ambassador of freedom loving people, Paul Robeson." She stood with the crowd and clapped her hands for what felt like an eternity. As her hands radiated heat, she took her seat with the hundreds in the audience. She closed her eyes as he began to speak, remembering the song he was best known for, "Old Man River." He spoke about the need for people not to give up on their dreams. He spoke about the need for the United States to set an example of freedom and to live up to its Constitution. Sharing with the crowds the trouble he had experienced from the government because he spoke out against racism, he reminded the crowd that nothing was impossible for them, if they set out to be honest, truthful and strong. "Never give up hope, never stop loving, and never stop believing in yourself."

She was not really aware when he stopped speaking. The whole thing was like a dream. It was as though time had stood still from the moment he had entered the room up until he left.

The memory of meeting this great Black man always stayed with Barbara. She later followed his life and paid attention whenever he was mentioned in the news. For many Blacks, he was their hero because he refused to allow the government to make him into their puppet. When they wanted him to turn in his friends and accuse them of Communism, he did not. And when they wanted him to sign a letter rejecting socialism and Communism, he also refused. Finally the government took away his passport, preventing him from traveling the world.

All her life, Barbara admired people who were courageous enough to speak the truth. It was one of her greatest joy to meet a man whom she admired, even though she learned most about how great he was after meeting him.

Like Truman, Paul Robeson reminded Barbara of the price one pays for standing up for justice. Later she would experience Christians threatening to kill her for speaking the truth and daring to be ordained a bishop.

Nationally, many things were in disarray. The government had raised taxes several times, cost of living was rising, labor unions encouraged workers to strike for their rights, and there was a lot of uncertainty in the world after the end of World War II. Soldiers had returned from the war with stories about planes, bombs, the fighting and a whole host of adventures. Some families had lost loved ones and people had tried to console these families in any way they could. With the passage of time, things got back to normal. People in Philadelphia faced a lot of uncertainties about the future and the Harris family was no exception.

It was in this climate of national and global uncertainties that Barbara graduated from high school. High school had been a lot of fun and Barbara had studied hard and partied hard. Every Friday night parents chaperoned the students at a friend's house and allowed them to dance and socialize until the wee hours of the morning. Barbara looked forward to these nights. Now that school was over, it was time to look for a job.

Living in a neighborhood like Germantown, word traveled easily about what was available in terms of work. Soon, Barbara heard about the possibility of working as a nurse's aide at one of the local hospitals. This certainly would not have been her first choice; she was not all that sure what exactly she wanted to do, but this was not it. But her parents always told her that sometimes you had to make the best of what was available until you got what you really wanted.

And so she reported for work, a little anxious but ready. Her title was "nurse's aide," which meant that the nurses could ask her to help out in any way possible. So sometimes she answered the phone and registered people, sometimes she helped the elderly fill out forms and explained to people what ailment they had. There were many days that she hated her job. At times, when she had to empty bedpans, she hoped that none of her high school classmates would see her at work. "Luckily," she thought to herself, "teenagers don't come to this place." The thought of being seen by some of her friends made her shiver. To add to her discomfort working at the hospital, the head nurse was very mean. Whenever Barbara had to talk to her or ask her a question an image of a bulldog came to mind. Sometimes Barbara had to force herself not to laugh as she spoke to her supervisor. The head nurse thought young people were soft and needed strict supervision and so she made it a point to be as harsh as possible with Barbara. When Barbara told her family about the woman, the general response was, "Don't let her get you down."

Hospital work demanded a lot of attention and focus, and Barbara found the work quite tiring. Another thing she was realizing was that working in a hospital meant that the patients always came first.

61

It was a hard reality to accept at times, especially when all she wanted to do was sit and eat her lunch.

One day as Barbara finally got a chance to sit down, she heard the sirens going off. She could distinguish when the siren was from an ambulance and when from a police or fire truck. The orderlies brought in a man who had been run over by a freight train. His face was twisted in pain, and his cries of anguish ripped through her body. She watched as the nurses attended him with such detachment. How do they do this? She asked herself. Good Lord, she knew she could not stick it out much longer here. "God, get me out of here," she prayed. The prayer had no sooner been uttered than the head nurse barked at her, "Young lady, get busy. We are not paying you to stand there and look pretty." Barbara felt her body cringing, but she controlled herself, said "Yes, Ma'am!" and went to find something to do. At times she would just walk around the floor, because apparently all the head nurse wanted was to see her moving.

Just when she thought that she was going to die from working as a nurse's aide, she heard about a job as a receptionist at a Children's Hospital. This made her very excited. She knew she would be good at it, because she loved answering the phone and connecting people. Her work involved greeting people as they came in, filling out forms, and directing them what to do until the doctor was ready to see them. A children's hospital was a fun place to be; there she saw many beautiful children. Barbara always loved children; they reminded her of her brother, Thomas. She treasured the days she spent reading to him, leading him around, and telling him how he should behave. And yet these children were sick—that was the only reason they came to the hospital. Her heart moved with compassion as she watched the sick children and the worried parents. She tried her best to cheer up the children. She wished she could heal them.

One day while at the front desk, the father of one of the boys she had dated and gone to dances with during high school walked in.

"Barbara, how are you doing?" he asked.

"I'm doing well, I like working here."

"You know, you should work for me!"

"Really? What kind of work do you have?"

"Well, I run a public relations firm and I think you would be good at it."

"Mmmm, let me think."

"What's there to think about? I think you are smart enough to do this work, I will pay you twenty-five dollars a week and there are a lot of things you will learn. And beyond that, you will help our community be a better place."

"Sounds great! I love it here, but you may be right. Let me talk to my family and get back to you."

Later that evening as the family gathered for dinner, Barbara told them about her conversation. Everybody was delighted. Three days later, Barbara called up the gentleman and told him that she would take the job.

And so began her career at Joseph V. Baker Associates, a national public relations firm, headquartered in Philadelphia. This was a Black-owned firm and within ten years she had risen to the position of president. In a man's world, she had succeeded and reached the top. Her work involved representing white companies in Black communities. She mastered her work and won high praise from her superiors and other members on her staff. Barbara stayed on at Baker Associates from 1949 to 1968

Later, she worked for Sun Oil Company as a public relations officer, where she became the department head. Barbara worked for Sun Oil from 1968 to 1980, and did not leave that position until after her ordination as a priest.

The little girl from Philadelphia who had surprised and delighted many at her birth, continued to surprise, delight, and at times shock many as her life unfolded. Barbara had worked hard and had become quite successful. All the while, she continued to find time to be with her family and to worship at St. Barnabas, the church where she was baptized.

63

◼

SIX

Making History: The Spirit of a Life

On Thursday, December 1, 1955, a Black woman named Rosa Parks refused to give up her seat to a white man. The segregation laws dictated that Blacks had to sit in the back of the bus if the bus was packed. If the bus was empty, Blacks could sit anywhere but had to give up their seat as soon as a white person entered the bus.

When Rosa Parks got on the bus, there were several vacant seats, so she sat in one of them closest to where the Blacks were ordered to sit. At the next stop some whites got on, they filled up all the seats, but one white man did not have a seat. On seeing this, the bus driver demanded that Rosa Parks give up her seat. She was so exhausted and so tired of segregation that she refused. Shortly after that, two policemen came on the bus and arrested her.

What seemed like a trivial incident mobilized many Blacks involved in the civil rights movement in America to change laws insisting whites be given preferential treatment. By taking a stand, this Black woman became part of a movement that changed the American racial and political landscape in a most dramatic way.

A similar thing happened to Barbara. She took a seat on the Episcopal Church's "bus." People wanted her to move, wanted her to obey rules about the roles of women in the church that she thought were outdated and un-Christian. She was not about to do what she knew in her heart was wrong. She took a seat in the church of the God she had known all her life, and there were many who wanted her to vacate the seat. She had been an Episcopalian all her life, and knew that she had as much right to be in the seat as anyone else. No matter the insults and the pain, she refused to give in to the stupidity and the arrogance of those in the church with a segregation mentality.

The United States in the 1960s and 1970s experienced a controversial time politically and religiously around the issues of race and equality. Race riots, lynching by the Ku-Klux-Klan, a white supremacist organization, and unending vicious debates among religious and political leaders threatened to rip the heart out of the country's belief in itself as a loving and tolerant society.

Philadelphia faced its share of racial discrimination, oppression, and racial advocacy. In 1967, when Barbara was only 37 years old, Black high school students demonstrated in front of the Board of Education. The police commissioner ordered the police forces to attack the Black students, dismantle the demonstration, leaving hundreds of young people bruised and battered. People thought the city would go up in flames, but nothing that violent happened. Brotherly love seemed to win out.

Brotherly love overcame violence with a little help from the Episcopal Church. During the 1960s, a very outspoken Black priest was in charge of one of the fastest growing Episcopal churches in Philadelphia. Paul Washington was known for his stance on civil rights and his outspoken advocacy on behalf of the rights of Black people. He was rector of the aptly named Church of the Advocate, and it was he who helped to soothe the angry crowd by opening up the church doors so they could be safe from the police and have a chance to speak.

After the riot of 1967, the Church of the Advocate took on national significance as a church committed to the plight of the poor. Paul Washington embraced a more radical living of the Gospel and invited Blacks of all persuasions to join his church. Once he preached that there were similarities among Blacks from the urban areas and the middle-class Blacks of Germantown. Little did he know that a woman from Germantown would come to his parish and not only change his parish, but the whole world.

A series of events came together in 1968 that were to change how the Americans and American churches viewed themselves. On April 4, 1968, a sniper assassinated Martin Luther King Jr. Barbara wept along with the rest of the world. Once again, she thought, we have killed a prophet.

He had advocated for the civil and human rights of all Americans and had called upon the churches to take a more prophetic stance towards the issues of justice. In addition, King preached a message of non-violent resistance. Unfortunately, after his death violence broke out, discrediting much of what he had advocated.

There was a noticeable difference between how Blacks connected to churches responded compared to Blacks who had no church affiliation. Amid the pain and agony, Blacks within the church found much comfort and encouragement from their religious leaders. There is no denying that one of the reasons racial tensions were different in Philadelphia was because so many Blacks attended church. When Martin Luther King, Jr. appeared on the national scene, many in Philadelphia appreciated his grounding his political struggles in the life and message of Jesus Christ. It was in the church that Blacks reinforced the fact that they were special and that God wanted them to live in freedom and peace. Blacks had the dual task of being faithful to God and loving all people in light of the reality of some their white fellow Christians treating them with hostility

So it is useful to keep in mind that Martin Luther King, Jr. was a contemporary of Barbara Harris. She had followed his life story, helped organize projects that supported his work, listened to his speeches, and marched part of the way from Selma to Montgomery, Alabama.

King's assassination led to riots throughout America including Philadelphia. Once again the Church of the Advocate offered itself and its resources as a calm within the storm. Paul Washington walked the streets like a modern day Jesus, calming the people and preventing further destruction.

Miles away in Germantown something was happening that would forever change the life of the Church of the Advocate. In April 1968, St. Barnabas, the church where Barbara had spent all her life, merged with St. Luke's, a larger white and Anglo-Catholic parish. Barbara had nothing in principle against the merger or the new congregation, but she found the liturgy too formal and detached from the reality she lived. She wanted to worship in a place that sang the spirituals, a place where everybody had a voice and where there was engagement in the struggle of the people.

Wandering around one Sunday she entered the Church of the Advocate. Walking up the aisle she was embraced by a stranger and led to a special seat. She did not need any more convincing that this was the church where God wanted her to be. What she did not know was that this church was about to lead her down a path she could never have imagined. She soon got to know the rector, Paul Washington, a lot better. They developed a great working relation-ship, and soon discovered they had many things in common. Paul became not only a great friend, but also a great mentor and pillar of strength.

In 1968, Barbara had been struggling to understand her own faith journey. What did it mean to follow Jesus in today's world? How does God want me to respond to the things around me?

Listening to the news and looking at the neighborhoods around her, Barbara believed that things could be different and better for all. She wanted to make sense of her call as a Christian in light of the harsh realities facing Blacks in Philadelphia and beyond. One could see the fear and the suffering in the lives of many Blacks in Philadelphia. This was a far cry from the idyllic childhood memories that Barbara had about her life in school and in church. It was not always easy for Barbara to reconcile her personal blessings and good fortune with the plight of so many of her brothers and sisters whose lives were being wasted by so much pain and suffering.

As the Civil Rights Movement took center stage in the American consciousness, many people turned to events in the church and tried to understand why there were so many disparities and inconsistencies in the Christian message.

"Here we are talking about equality, yet many of us in the church do not have a voice. We still live in a male dominated church," Barbara said at one of the church's vestry meetings.

It is only fair to say that Barbara and her family did not always support the rights of women. The movement for women's rights was still not popular in many circles. People who grew up in the church prided themselves on following tradition. So the path to believing that women could be priest was a slow one for Barbara and even slower for her mother. It was a case of experience being the best teacher, because Barbara used her experience in the working world and conversations with women in the church to come to believe that God made no distinctions based on race, gender, or age.

Whereas the Episcopal Church was not explicitly racist in its actions, it certainly discriminated against women. Barbara, who in her secular job had to contend with men who thought women were not as qualified, showed them that she was just as qualified and talented, if not more so. She felt that women in the church were being given the bad end of the bargain because of the laws in the church that restricted most of the leadership to men.

"I am very passionate about these issues. We must bring about full inclusion of all peoples into the church, eradicate racism, and get rid of sexism. We must use the influence of the church to address some of the issues in our society, issues of economic injustice, equal opportunity, quality education for all people, housing and homelessness."

At the Episcopal Church's General Convention of 1970, a resolution to admit women to the priesthood failed. In 1973, the resolution failed again; in fact it got fewer votes than it did in 1970.

Many parishioners at the Church of the Advocate, where Barbara attended church during the 1970s, were upset about the church's refusal to ordain women. Barbara was a vestry member at that time, and many people sought her out to talk about what was happening in the church.

She comforted the parishioners by reminding them that their freedom as Black people had come after many years and at great cost. At one of the many meetings at the church to talk about the ordination of women, Barbara stood in their midst and spoke to them of all the things that had happened in the struggle for justice and equality.

Beginning with the experience of slavery and the movement for women's rights, she drew parallels to the civil rights movement, assuring them that justice and truth often took a long time to be realized.

She helped the people see that women and Blacks did not always have equal opportunity under the law. Barbara reminded them about their experiences of civil disobedience in order to obtain equality under the law. People listened carefully to what she said. They punctuated a lot of what she said with loud calls of "Amen" and "Tell it sister!" and "That's right!"

Could God be calling women and men in the church to disobey certain church laws? Her words burned within them as they recalled their own struggles for justice and acceptance.

During this time, Suzanne Hiatt, a friend and mentor of Barbara's and longtime parishioner at the Church of the Advocate, worked actively to realize her dream of being ordained a priest.

Sue was a deacon at the time. On June 15, 1974, a Dean of the Philadelphia Divinity School called for the ordination of women priests in a homily delivered at the school. The retired bishop said the time had come for women to be ordained as priests. He called for prophetic and courageous people to bring about the birth of a new way of being God's people.

Sue was impressed. A bishop was echoing her thoughts and the thoughts of her parish in Philadelphia.

Sue called her rector, Paul Washington, Barbara, and a few bishops. Sue wanted action. She knew a few women around the country who would follow her and take the bold step in breaking with tradition.

In 1974, history was changed forever in the Anglican Communion. On July 29 of that year, three retired bishops ordained eleven women deacons to the priesthood. The female priests became known as the "Philadelphia 11." Barbara was not one of them, but she was part of a group of bishops, deacons, and lay people that met privately to plan the ordinations.

The group wanted to make sure that the women who wanted to be ordained were contacted and had all the information they needed. It was also necessary to work out the details of the service and ensure that all necessary plans for the ordination were in place. Three bishops would have to do the ordination, and the group wanted to ensure that the events would proceed safely and without problems.

For the ordinations, they decided on July 29, the feast day of Mary and Martha.

Word spread about the ordination plans. Many bishops throughout America objected to it. The Presiding Bishop, the head of the Episcopal Church in America, urged the group not to go ahead with the ordination. He had the power to recommend what should be done, but he had no power to stop the ordination. Even, the Archbishop of Canterbury, the head of all the Anglicans and Episcopalians who form the Anglican Communion, tried to persuade them not to go ahead with the ordination.

The eleven women received letters of warning and even threats. Many supportive letters were also received, and there were more voices in favor of the ordination than against it.

Everyone involved in the planning of the ordination knew that what they were about to do would change the Anglican Communion forever.

"Barbara, would you be willing to carry the cross ahead of the procession into the church?" a member of the planning team asked.

"That's a great idea!" the others chimed in.

Barbara sat still for a few moments.

"I think I can do that," she said. "Oh yes, I would love to."

"We have received some threats, so we won't be able to process outside the church," someone said.

During the days leading up to the ordination, Barbara was not in Philadelphia. She had wanted to be there but had to go to San Francisco to attend a business conference. Miles away, her mind was on her friends at the Church of the Advocate. She prayed for them. "Yes", she said, "I have to keep all those women, all those people and the whole church in my heart."

She kept in contact with her rector and friend, Paul Washington. She worried about him. The bishops who would ordain the women were retired, the women to be ordained would one day gain acceptance, but Paul Washington could lose his job and lose his church community because of participating in this ordination. So she prayed especially for him.

Sometime before the day of the ordination, she called him to check in. She wanted to make sure that he was holding up and doing all right.

"Paul?"

"Barbara! We all wish you were here now."

"Is the ordination still on?" she asked him.

"Oh Barbara, you know it is," he said, "so just get on that plane and come on down, 'cause you are going to lead the procession into the church."

"All right, now. Don't you worry, I wouldn't miss it for all the tea in China."

Barbara had advocated on behalf of these women, supported them, and had prayed that the day would come when women would be ordained priests. That day was fast approaching. Angry men and women had been calling her and some even threatened her. But she was not afraid.

Barbara believed that the hand of God was a part of writing this new history in the life of the church.

"You people will cause a split in the church," an old woman said to Barbara.

"The church is already split," Barbara said, "and that is why we are ordaining these women."

"Even if you all paid me, I won't be showing up in that church!"

"That's all right. God will show up. The time has come and it will be done. Those women will be ordained."

On the day of the ordination hundreds of people came out to celebrate the ordination of the eleven women. Some people gathered outside the Church of the Advocate to protest and pray. These people felt that the Episcopal Church would be destroyed forever if women were ordained priests because they thought it was going against God's will.

Inside the church, people applauded, danced, shouted "Amen!" and offered up thanksgiving prayers to God for the eleven women. When the bishops started up the aisle, people applauded. The service took place without any major problems. After three hours of singing, listening to readings, and prayers, the Episcopal Church had its first women priests.

Moonlight gave the evening a special glow, a bird chirped in the distance, and a gentle wind blew through the trees. It was a great night for thinking, Barbara reflected. Piece by piece she went over all the events that had led up to the day's events. They brought a smile to her face.

She had led the eleven women into the church. Might God be asking her to lead women and men, clergy and lay, Black and white, all peoples into a new experience of the church? Could God be calling her to be a priest?

As she returned to her daily occupation, Barbara pondered these questions and the events of the day in her heart.

Barbara continued to find life, love, and fellowship in her congregation. In some ways, the Church of the Advocate reminded her of the joy and the comfort that she felt as a child listening to her mother play the organ in church.

On the roof of the church was a statue of the angel, Gabriel. Long before Barbara had become a member in the church she had heard of "the church with the angel on top." Barbara never entered the church without looking up at Gabriel. She knew that it was the angel Gabriel God sent to Mary to announce that she would give birth to the Savior. This angel was the bearer of Good News. On the days when she arrived early for meetings, she would look up at the angel and ask jokingly, "So Gabriel, when will you bring me some good news?"

Barbara continued her work at the church. She devoted more time to her church community, but still experienced a desire to do something different. In prayer she sensed God had something in store for her.

At times she ignored and resisted the call and tried not to think about it. There were days when the idea of being a priest seemed a good idea. It felt right, sometimes. And there were days when she felt nervous and afraid about the whole thing.

But the call to ordained ministry never diminished. She confided in a friend asking, "How can this be?" The friend responded, "God does not call those who are worthy. God makes worthy those whom God would call." The clouds lifted. It was clear to Barbara that God was calling her to ministry.

That night, she asked God, "Are you crazy?" Barbara did not expect an answer to this question, but an answer came and she heard it. Somewhere deep in her soul, she heard the answer from God: "Yes."

A calm descended on her at that moment, tears rolled down her cheeks and she laughed joyously. Her heart was at peace and she knew without a doubt that God had been calling her all along to ordained ministry.

Once it was clear to Barbara that God was calling her to be a priest, she never looked back. Like all new decisions, she was faced with the task of figuring out how to get it done.

One of Barbara's early mottos was that God could provide a way out of no way. She had confidence in God's grace. She was no longer afraid.

While working full time, she made the effort to begin her theological preparations for the priesthood. In 1976, she enrolled at Metropolitan Collegiate Center in Philadelphia and later took courses at Villanova University, Philadelphia and in Sheffield, England.

Barbara sometimes wondered about the importance of some of the things she was studying. Theological studies at times seemed so far removed from the work she did at the Church of the Advocate.

She was often tired, overworked, and felt discouraged, but she was determined to finish her studies. Many nights, she was up late studying. Whenever she saw something she liked or found puzzling she would write it down. "I have to think about that," she would say or "Maybe, I will use that later."

Her mentor and rector, Paul Washington, stood by and encouraged her. The more he watched her dedication to the task of becoming a priest, the more he became convinced that God had great things in store for her.

Barbara's family and best friends from high school called regularly and told her that they were praying for her. She was happy to know that people believed in her call to the ordained ministry. At the family cookout, Barbara told her mother about her studies. Her mother did not believe that women should be priests and she often said it to Barbara. But they understood each other and her mother kept saying, "I love you and I always trust your judgment."

In 1979, she was ordained a deacon, and, in October 1980, Barbara Clementine Harris was ordained a priest. Both ordinations happened at the Church of the Advocate.

In 1984, the Rev. Barbara Harris became the executive director of the Episcopal Church Publishing Company and publisher of *The Witness*. She wrote many articles about life in the Episcopal Church and for all those who, for whatever reasons, felt excluded from society and the life of the church. Barbara was not afraid to criticize those with whom she disagreed, even if it was the President of the United States, and she often did.

73

As a priest, Barbara continued to speak out against racism, sexism, and other injustices in society. She believed that if one person suffers, everyone suffers. She devoted a lot of her energy to the Union of Black Episcopalians and the Episcopal Urban Caucus, church organizations concerned with social justice.

Barbara felt a special call to bring good news to those in prisons. She chose Bible passages carefully, because she wanted the inmates to know that God loved and still cared for them. At the Philadelphia County Prison, she counseled the prisoners and worshiped with them. She always had a joke for them; they loved her and were surprised at how funny she was. Soon they started to tell her jokes. The prisoners encouraged her in her priesthood and taught her a lot about the freedom of the human spirit.

Some called Barbara a rabble-rouser, because they found her views controversial. She wrote many articles about racism, the treatment of women and gays, and the response to the poor in the Episcopal Church. Because of her articles and sermons, some people argued that she was a left-wing fanatic, a troublemaker, and many other unflattering things.

Many readers, Episcopalians and non-Episcopalians, supported her, writing letters agreeing with her positions. For so many Episcopalians she was the voice of hope, the voice of one crying out for justice and at the same time proclaiming Good News.

In the 1980s, there had been a lot of talk about the possibility of a woman bishop. Most of the conversations focused on the following questions: Since women finally had been ordained priests, what would prevent them from being ordained bishops? Could women be made bishops? If we are all one in Christ Jesus, why should women be excluded?

Like the debates of the 1970s, the whole Anglican Communion debated these questions in the family dining room, during vestry meetings, at conventions, on television and at conferences throughout the world. People wrote papers, letters, seminars, and books for and against the ordination of women as bishops.

Many men and women, clergy and lay, spoke boldly, saying that since all are baptized in Jesus, all have equal share in the ministries of the church. This, they said, would strengthen the church and represent God's unconditional love.

Those who did not agree said that there was a need to hold to the tradition of male bishops. Women indeed followed Jesus, but only men were chosen as apostles. To ordain female bishops would only cause further divisions in the Anglican Communion.

Barbara continued preaching at the Church of the Advocate in Philadelphia. She constantly reminded the congregation that there was no turning back the hands of time and the work of God. "In God," she loved to remind the congregation, "there is neither Jew nor Greek, Black or white, male or female, slave or free." This was one of her favorite quotations from Paul.

As a priest who supported the ordination of women as bishops, Barbara always felt that when the time came, a white woman would be made a bishop. Most of the female priests in the Episcopal Church were white and held most of the important jobs. For this reason, Barbara felt that a white woman would be the first female Episcopal bishop. This is what she believed and of course she was not afraid of stating her views publicly.

—■——■

Lambeth Conferences, held every ten years, are gatherings of all bishops of the national churches within the Anglican Communion at which matters of common concern are discussed and decisions about policies are made. In 1988, the most divisive topic at Lambeth was whether to ordain women as bishops. Up to that point, many dioceses throughout the world still had not ordained women as priests.

A majority of the American bishops and other representatives made it clear that they were in favor of the ordination of women as priests and bishops.

It was decided that dioceses could ordain women bishops at their choosing, but the Lambeth Conference was not willing to endorse this position. Allowing women to be ordained as bishops was viewed as having the potential to create division or lead to many leaving the Anglican Communion.

In 1987, the Massachusetts delegates at a convention in Boston had recommended that Bishop Johnson, the diocesan bishop, receive additional support. The Episcopal Diocese of Massachusetts is the largest diocese in the United States and the delegates felt that Bishop Johnson needed help in carrying out his mission as bishop.

The time had come to elect an assistant bishop. Waiting until after the Lambeth Conference of 1988, the Diocese was now ready to focus its energy on electing a suffragan bishop. Suffragan bishop is the name given to a bishop who assists the chief bishop of a diocese.

A nominating committee was formed and the members carefully examined the process for receiving names of possible bishops and the work involved in learning about the candidates. About six months later, there were six nominees for the suffragan bishop and the Reverend Barbara Clementine Harris was one of them.

As was the custom, the nominees went throughout the diocese for three days answering questions and getting to know the people in Massachusetts. This was an ideal chance for the clergy and laity to get to know the candidates for suffragan bishop.

Barbara Harris was not the only woman and not the only Black candidate, but she spoke with a passion that soon set her apart from the others. At times her responses were so funny that it took minutes for people to stop laughing.

The more questions she answered, the more she was asked. She seemed comfortable and brave, and in the face of the toughest questions never lost her sense of humor or her ability to speak in terms that everyone could understand.

All the candidates participated in these get-to-know-you sessions throughout the diocese. She attracted the most attention because people either loved or hated her answers. Some people thought that she was too radical. Others thought that she might be too controversial. Some asked, would she be too confrontational, too outspoken and divisive? Others wondered, is she the best candidate for the diocese now? Many grumbled against her saying that she was a Black woman, had been divorced, and did not have enough theological training.

Something about the way Barbara talked about God, her life, her vision of the church, and justice made her quite popular with many of the people at the interview sessions. She spoke with authority and all were amazed at her wisdom.

Two weeks later, on September 24, 1988, five hundred delegates gathered at the Cathedral Church of St. Paul in downtown Boston. The time had come to elect a suffragan bishop for the diocese.

Barbara was at home in Philadelphia with a few friends who had gathered that day to keep her company.

Bishop Johnson, in his opening remarks, asked the delegates "to be available to God's presence. That what we do may truly be the expression of God's will and not an expression solely of our own."

When the Reverend Mary Glasspool, a priest from Philadelphia who was working in Boston at the time, nominated Barbara Harris before the delegates, she shook with excitement as she said, "She may at times make us uncomfortable about the way things are—but that is precisely what Jesus did. He made the religious people of his time uncomfortable and when they responded to his vision, they did so by changing their lives. We have a rare opportunity to be the first, with the blessings of God's Holy Spirit, to realize unity in diversity, thereby moving us closer to the reign of God."

Barbara Harris and the Reverend Marshall Hunt were the crowd favorites, with most people expecting Hunt to win easily. Hunt had been the stewardship consultant for ten years and was quite popular among the clergy in Massachusetts.

There were four women in Germantown, Philadelphia for whom the events of the day held special interest. They had gathered to offer support, encouragement and presence to one another. Barbara Harris, her sister, her best friend, and a priest from Philadelphia working in Washington talked, laughed, and listened to each other. Barbara's best friend, Gayle Harris is now suffragan bishop in the Diocese of Massachusetts.

They were happy together. Over many years they had developed the strong bond of friendship and love. Sometimes, they said nothing and a silence descended upon them. Eventually, Barbara would launch into a story and soon all the women would start laughing. They would hold their sides and beg her to stop telling funny stories.

Hundreds of miles away in Boston, Massachusetts, there was another gathering. Over five hundred delegates had gathered to choose a suffragan bishop. People all over the country wondered whether Massachusetts would be the first diocese to elect a woman bishop. Some thought it would never happen, while some believed that it was possible.

Back in Philadelphia, the women talked about what it would be like when the Episcopal Church elected a woman bishop. Barbara reminded them of the ordination of women fourteen years ago. "You never know what new thing God is capable of doing," she said. As soon as she spoke these words, the sun moved from behind the clouds and filled the room with light. Then there was silence, four friends looking at each other and just enjoying one another's company.

"Are you nervous?" one of them asked, looking at her watch.

"Not really, I feel quite calm," Barbara replied. "When the phone rings, I will know the answer. In the meantime, could you pass me some cheese and crackers?"

"It's too much. I can't take the tension anymore," Barbara's sister said, walking towards another room.

"Josephine, don't be worried or upset, just believe that everything's in God's hands," Barbara said, going over to stand next to her sister.

"Barbara, can I get you anything?" another of the women asked.

"Pour me another drink. Something refreshing is in order," Barbara said.

They all laughed.

In the meantime, the delegates were approaching another round of voting. Bishop Johnson, the Bishop of Massachusetts, read the results from the last ballot and asked the delegates to vote again. It was obvious that the race was between two candidates, but neither had sufficient votes to be declared a winner.

People began to wonder how many ballots they would need before knowing who will be the next bishop. It was a tight race. Would the man win or would the woman?

A nominee needed a majority of votes from the clergy and from the lay delegates. Women and men were crying tears of joy and hope, as they told others why they thought Barbara was worth their vote. But supporters of the other nominees also worked hard to convince delegates to vote for their candidates.

Barbara had a good chance, but it was still close. Her supporters gave each other the thumbs-up; they would keep lobbying for her. Delegates knew who they needed to target to convince.

Hunt increased his lead on the second ballot and almost sealed the election on the third ballot. On the third ballot, he won a majority of the lay votes and only needed five more to win the clergy votes.

78

"Thank God," one priest said. "Let some other diocese create history. We don't want any women bishop here."

"Don't rejoice, yet," a male delegate said to him, "Barbara will be our next bishop. I can feel it."

Lobbying became more intense. Vying parties knew that a great deal was at stake. Some male priests were working hard to ensure that a woman would not become a bishop in Massachusetts. They wanted to send a message to the rest of the country and the world. But others believed that baptism made all Christians children of God and that Barbara would be a great bishop, so they rallied to convince others of how important it was to elect Barbara.

Each successive ballot Barbara inched closer and closer, cutting Hunt's margin. On the fourth ballot, Barbara moved ahead in the clergy votes, and her lead kept growing, and by the fifth ballot those who supported Barbara felt a lot more hopeful. A dream might become reality.

Women and men, priests and laity wanted a church where women were equal. They were convinced that it was possible and had spent many days calling other delegates and saying why they thought Barbara was a good candidate.

After each vote, people whispered and talked. As Barbara's chances increased people started clapping after the votes were announced.

Some sat on the edge of their seats, some stood up, some whispered, some bit their fingernails, others prayed, and one woman kept her eyes on the cross. Then there was silence.

They were nearing the sixth ballot.

Not everybody looked favorably on the possibility of creating history. A priest pointing to the heavens ripped his clothes and screamed, "You will destroy the church! Jesus never wanted women to be bishops. You must stop this madness!" An old Black woman handed him a yellow rose and gave him a big bear hug. For a brief moment, he was calm, but he stormed out of the cathedral and never returned.

A few minutes later, Bishop Johnson stood up, a serious look on his face. He had to cancel the sixth ballot, he said. When the delegates had heard this, they were deeply shaken. A united gasp went up from the delegates. What could this mean?

People started shouting. Bishop Johnson asked the delegates for their attention. He believed that some delegates had voted early. No one wanted this to be an election with any doubts attached to it, so it was seen as a wise decision to cancel the sixth ballot.

The convention took a break for lunch. Some wanted to keep lobbying, because much was at stake, but many went off to pray and listen to the Holy Spirit.

After lunch, there was a seventh ballot. It confirmed that Barbara Clementine Harris was on her way to creating history. The clergy vote for Hunt had eroded and Barbara was in need of only three lay votes to win.

The delegates voted an eighth time. When the eighth ballot was done the final tally read Harris 145 clergy and 136 lay votes—more than enough to win.

Bishop Johnson stood up and announced, "We have a bishop!"

The delegates elected Barbara.

"A miracle, thank God," a woman proclaimed, "My eyes have seen the glory of the Lord revealed today."

"Oh, my God, oh God, oh God, praise God," a woman kept repeating through her sobs.

The cathedral erupted into a joyful noise, shaking the building's foundations. With exultant and sincere hearts, many gave loud praises to God. People wept, sang glory to God, laughed, danced and applauded.

A loud voice was heard from someone in the gathering, "This is my beloved daughter with whom I am well pleased." Some people stormed out of the church, refusing to accept that Barbara Harris, a woman, had been voted suffragan bishop.

Bishop Johnson asked for calm. He wanted to address the convention, but it took a long time for people to settle down. They were excited. When they finally quieted down, he asked all the delegates to treat this historic moment with love and sensitivity. He said a prayer and asked the congregation to sing the hymn: *The Church's One Foundation*.

The day had been long, filled with both tension and excitement. Finally, the election was over. The Episcopal Diocese of Massachusetts had elected a suffragan bishop. Bishop Johnson asked for calm, he said a few words of thanks for all the delegates, and excused himself in order to go and make a phone call. He wanted to share the good news with Barbara.

Back in Philadelphia, the phone rang. The women froze and looked over at the ringing phone. It rang again. No one moved. It rang a third time.

"Ok, I'll get it," Barbara said, motioning her friends to gather round the phone. "Hello."

"Hello, Barbara?"

"Yes…yes…yes…This is she!" Barbara replied.

"This is Bishop Johnson."

"It's Bishop Johnson," Barbara whispered to the women.

"The Diocese just elected you suffragan bishop."

"Oh my God, oh my God, oh my God" the other women shouted. They jumped and danced all over the room.

"Ladies, I can't hear the bishop," she said, a wide smile forming on her face. She brought the phone close to her face and looked into the eyes of her friends and said, "I humbly accept."

After she hung up the phone the women embraced her as they all cried and laughed. Then one of the women left the room and Barbara followed her. They stood looking at each other.

"Oh my God," Barbara's sister said, "Congratulations! You are the first woman bishop. Bishop Barbara Clementine Harris."

"I can't believe it, either!" Barbara said. They hugged each other and walked out to join the others.

Barbara laughed. She reached over and touched her best friends' shoulders.

"I forgot that I was not to say *I accept*. I was to say, *I will pray about it and see if it is God's will*."

She paused for a while and said, "I like what I said. I accept."

Evening was approaching, but it was the dawning of a new day in the church and the world.

It had happened, Barbara Clementine Harris was elected a bishop, the first woman in the world to receive this honor.

The next step was to receive a majority of votes from bishops and dioceses of the Episcopal Church. The results came in slowly, but when the results were tallied, there was no doubt that Barbara Clementine Harris would be the first female bishop in the Anglican Communion.

Epilogue

As the day of consecration came near, devout
Christians from other denominations, dignitaries, and well wishers
of every nation, color, and persuasion under heaven gathered in
Boston. Throughout the Diocese, people prepared for this great
event. Many said it was a new birth for the church; a new Pentecost.

The attention of the world focused upon Barbara and Boston as
the day drew nearer. Indeed, many felt they were living in a time of
the fulfillment of scriptures, "in Christ, there is no Jew nor Greek,
no male or female."

On February 11, 1988 the sun shone brightly and the clouds
looked like angels on Jacob's ladder. A large flock of doves flew over
the Cathedral Church of St. Paul and disappeared from sight.

So many were those who wanted to come the diocese decided to
find a space much bigger than the Cathedral Church of St. Paul.
They selected a convention center in Boston, large enough to seat
all those expected to attend.

At the Hynes Convention Center before 8,000 people, many
bishops, many women priests, many African Americans, and a
whole host of people of good will, Barbara Clementine Harris was
consecrated Suffragan Bishop of the Diocese of Massachusetts.

Never before in the history of the Episcopal Church had there
been a gathering so festive, so colorful, and so joyous. For forty-five
minutes acolytes, guests, civic leaders, and 1,200 priests and bishops
processed into the church, rocking and swaying as the choirs sang
the music of Gabrieli and Handel, Mozart and the spirituals, *In Dat*

Great Getting' Up Mornin' and *Ride on, King Jesus*. When the crowd caught sight of her entering the auditorium the whole room rose in a thunderous and joyful standing ovation. Barbara Harris turned to her friend, Canon Ed Rodman, a priest in the Diocese of Massachusetts, and said to him, "What a hell of a welcome."

The Presiding Bishop, Edmond Lee Browning, was the chief consecrating bishop, and he was joined by many bishops from the United States and other countries. The Rev. Li Tim Oi from China, the first woman ordained a priest in the Anglican Communion participated in the Eucharist.

As is the custom, the Presiding Bishop gave an opportunity for those who did not agree with the ordination of Barbara to express their dissent. You could feel the silence.

For a few moments nothing happened. Then heads started turning. A man was heading toward an open mike. People started whispering to each other; they knew the man. He was a priest who had been against the ordination of female bishops.

Some in the crowd started to shout as a way of preventing him from speaking. Bishop Browning asked for silence. Barbara kept her eyes focused on the cross. She never looked at him.

He held the mike tightly, twisting it. Then he screamed, "This is a farce! You are not a priest, not a bishop, and no sacraments that you perform will be legitimate. I call on the Presiding Bishop not to go ahead with this pretended ordination."

As the man continued to speak the crowd got restless. But they had expected this. The man continued to quote from the canons and the scriptures why Barbara should not be made a bishop.

As he spoke, an elderly Black woman got out of her seat. She was well dressed and wore a beautiful hat. She straightened it and left her seat.

"That's Barbara's mother," someone whispered. "I wonder what she is going to do."

Walking over to Barbara she hugged her and said, "Don't worry my child. It will be all right. I am your mother and I know." As soon as the women hugged each other, the man stopped talking and went back to his seat.

Bishop Browning stood up and said, "A majority of bishops have approved the ordination and we have followed the correct procedures. It is of God. Let us proceed." The church stood and applauded joyfully.

Soon all the bishops present came forward to lay their hands on Barbara Clementine Harris following a very ancient tradition that for thousands of years was only done for men.

The bishops then moved back to their positions. Standing like a bright sun on a cloudy day, Barbara was dressed in her miter and the vestments of a bishop. It was the first time a woman had worn a miter and held the bishop's staff in the history of the Anglican Church.

She looked radiant, confident and looked right. "The Miter Fits Just Fine," a newspaper headline read the next day. It was one of the things Barbara said that day. "The miter fits fine." And it did.

The girl from Germantown was the new bishop in the Anglican Communion.

Since that Great Getting' Up Mornin', February 11, 1988, the Rt. Rev. Barbara Clementine Harris, the courageous little girl from Philadelphia, has stood as an icon, a beacon of hope, a voice for justice, and a clear sign that God dwells among us.

Bishop Harris holds a vision of God's reign for all peoples with music in her heart. She invites all people to follow God, invites the church to walk with her, and promises that you can sing along with one of her favorite songs:

> I'm pressing on the upward way,
> New heights I'm gaining every day
> Still praying as I onward bound,
> 'Lord plant my feet on higher ground.'
> For faith has caught a joyful sound.
> The song of saints on higher ground.
> Lord lift me up, and let me stand
> By faith on heaven's table land
> A higher plain that I have found,
> Lord plant my feet on higher ground.

85

Bishop Barbara Clementine Harris worked hard all her life, but she worked especially hard on behalf of justice, equal rights for all, and for a church where all are respected and loved. She has had rough days, and the battle at times has been fierce. Some bishops and lay people in the world still revile her, accuse and falsely say all manner of evil against her. She has had to learn how to be wise as a serpent and gentle as a dove. She has continued her commitment to the professional and community organizations she holds dear. Bishop Harris has continued to find life and grace in her parish visits. She has continued to prophesy. These are words she repeats quite often in her travels:

"The world today is looking for truth; it is looking for justice; it is looking for those who have compassion, yea even more for those who are willing to demonstrate their faith and their conviction by being examples of that which we profess. No one expects us to eliminate all of the evil of the world, nor to liberate all those who are oppressed, nor to feed all who are hungry or to house the millions who are homeless. But when the oppressed see one who fights for liberation, their burden is lightened because they know that somebody cares. When the victims of injustice see one who is fighting for justice, their suffering is a little less painful because they know that somebody cares. When the world sees one who takes a righteous stand and is willing to be persecuted for righteousness sake, it knows that somebody cares."